All Profits to Charity

By purchasing this book, you're not only gaining valuable insights into retirement and real estate but also making a meaningful difference in our community. All profits will be donated to the Victoria Women's Transition House, which provides safe shelter, counselling, and support to women and children facing intimate partner violence. Your support benefits both your future and those in need today.

Disclosure:

This book is intended to share general ideas to help you think about how real estate may fit into your retirement plans. However, every individuals financial situation, goals, and tax considerations are unique. You should always consult qualified professionals, including a financial advisor, tax accountant, lawyer, and real estate expert before making any decisions. The author does not endorse or promote any specific financial advisor, and readers are encouraged to conduct their own due diligence when selecting professionals. Certain strategies discussed, including the use of leverage, carry significant risk and may not be suitable for all investors. Such strategies should only be considered with the guidance of a qualified professional, who understands your full financial picture. In addition, tax laws are complex and subject to change; always consult a qualified tax professional before making any tax related decisions.

FROM REAL ESTATE TO RETIREMENT:

Rethink, Retire, and Thrive

CLAYTON MEERES

Dedication

This book is dedicated to all Canadians who believe that their real estate shouldn't just be a line item on their net worth statement but rather a powerful tool to help them achieve what's most important to them sooner and with greater peace of mind.

Table of Contents

"Most people spend their lives climbing the ladder of success, only to realize when they reach the top, they had it against the wrong wall."
- Stephen R. Covey.

Introduction:

Rethink Real Estate, Retire with Confidence

Not long ago, I was meeting with a friend, Jake Miller. Jake is a successful custom home builder and real estate investor, someone I've known for years. Over coffee, we chatted about the challenges we each faced in our respective fields, and, of course, we ended up talking about our clients and how we can help them navigate the complex financial decisions that come their way.

As the conversation turned to retirement planning, I mentioned an idea I had for a book called From Real Estate to Retirement—a guide designed to help Canadians understand how to optimize their real estate as part of their retirement strategy.

Without missing a beat, Jake let out a frustrated sigh and muttered, almost to himself, "I'd buy that."

I was a little taken aback. "What do you mean?" I asked, genuinely curious. I'd always assumed that someone as successful in real estate as Jake would have a clear plan for retirement—not be uncertain about it.

Jake leaned back in his chair, rubbing his forehead. "Well, to be honest, I've spent so much time building my real estate business, and the idea of unwinding it all? It feels overwhelming. I've put it off because, frankly, I don't know where to even begin. The thing is, I've focused all my resources on how to build wealth. But no one talks about what to do when you're at the stage of actually using that wealth for retirement. I don't know what I need to know or what decisions I should be making. It'd be great to have a resource that helps me understand the stages of this process that I can trust."

I nodded. Jake's concern is one I've heard time and again from clients who've spent years building their real estate portfolios but never quite figured out how to incorporate those assets into their retirement planning.

For decades, retirement planning has focused primarily on pensions, savings, and investments—things like RRSPs, TFSAs, and mutual funds—but it overlooks something incredibly important: real estate.

For most Canadians, real estate is often the single largest asset they'll have in retirement. Yet, despite its size and significance, very few people know how to optimize this asset as they prepare to retire. I decided to write this book to create a practical, straightforward guide that helps Canadians navigate the real estate decisions they need to make before and during retirement.

Whether it's deciding when to sell, how to use rental income, or how to avoid unnecessary tax penalties, the journey from real estate to retirement doesn't need to be a complicated one. But it does require thoughtful planning, and that's what From Real Estate to Retirement is all about: providing clarity, actionable steps, and peace of mind during every stage of the process.

Why Real Estate is The Missing Piece in Retirement Planning

Canada is undergoing a massive demographic shift. With more than nine million Canadians over the age of 65—representing nearly a quarter of the country's population—retirement planning has never been more important. The choices retirees make about their real estate today will have a lasting impact on their financial security and quality of life in the years ahead.

In cities like, but not limited to, Vancouver, Toronto, and Victoria, property values have surged, leaving many retirees house-rich but cash-poor. Some want to stay in their homes but need better financial strategies. Others want to relocate to a lower-cost area but aren't sure where to start. And for those with investment properties, the challenge becomes deciding whether to continue managing tenants or cash out.

Retirement isn't just about money. It's also about simplifying your lifestyle and finding financial security and freedom. And for most Canadians, housing plays a central role in that equation.

How to Use This Book

Think of this book as a roadmap for real estate decisions and your retirement. You don't have to read it cover to cover—just jump to the section that matters most to you. If you're a few years away from retirement and want to know if you should be optimizing or preparing better, start there. If you're already retired and wondering whether to downsize, jump straight to that section. If you're thinking about passing your property to the next generation or minimizing taxes, go directly to those chapters first.

Use this book in a way that makes the most sense for your situation—whether that means reading it cover to cover, flipping to the chapters that answer your biggest questions, or even handing it off to someone who's at a crossroads and doesn't know which path to take.

This isn't a one-size-fits-all solution. Every retiree's situation is different. But my goal is to help you think about your real estate wealth in a new way, as a flexible tool you can use at different stages, rather than something that simply is, and must be dealt with later.

What This Book Will Help You Achieve

Rethink: Most people view their home as just a place to live, but in reality, it's one of the most powerful financial tools they own. In this book, you'll learn how to rethink real estate as an integral part of your retirement plan that can enhance your financial security rather than limit it. You'll gain clarity on how to make real estate decisions based on values and logic, not emotion, and how to align those decisions with your long-term goals. Whether you're considering downsizing, renting out a portion of your home, or keeping your property for the next generation, you'll learn how to evaluate your options with confidence and purpose.

Retire: With this new perspective, you'll be able to craft a retirement strategy that works for you rather than feeling trapped by your home. You'll discover how to turn real estate wealth into a reliable income stream, reduce tax inefficiencies, and ensure your housing choices support your financial freedom instead of hindering it. By understanding how to optimize your assets based on which stage of retirement you're in, you'll be able to retire with more control, flexibility, and peace of mind.

Thrive: True financial freedom is about living a retirement that aligns with your values and priorities, not just about having enough money. This book will help you shift from simply maintaining a home to building a lifestyle that allows you to enjoy your wealth, pursue your passions, and leave a meaningful legacy. Whether that means travelling, spending more time with family, or supporting causes that matter to you, you'll be equipped with the knowledge and strategies to thrive in retirement, knowing your home and investments are working for you—not the other way around.

Stage 1:

Preparing for Retirement - Unlocking Your Wealth

"When your values are clear,
the decision is easy."
- Roy Disney.

Chapter 1:

If You're Stuck, Start Here

Asking the Right Questions to Make the Best Decisions

Have you ever felt like financial advice was being sold to you rather than designed for you? That's exactly how I felt in my early twenties when I walked into my bank. Instead of asking about my goals or priorities, the advisor spent the first ten minutes promoting a financial product they were selling. When he finally finished, I asked, "That's great, but what does any of that have to do with what's important to me?" He had no answer.

That experience stuck with me and shaped how I approach financial planning today. Every financial decision, especially one as significant as how to use real estate in retirement, should be rooted in what truly matters to you.

The Values Ladder: Aligning Money with What Truly Matters

One of the most effective ways to make informed financial decisions is by understanding what truly matters to you. Whether working through this alone or with a financial advisor, the key question to ask yourself is: **What's important about money to me?**

This is not about right or wrong answers—it's about exploring your priorities. Some people may have a single-word response, while others may need a deep conversation to uncover their core values. The most effective way to do this is through a simple yet powerful exercise called the Values Ladder.

The concept of aligning financial decisions with personal values is inspired by Bill Bacharach, the creator of Values-Based Financial Planning. His work has shaped the way I approach financial conversations, ensuring that decisions aren't just about numbers but about what truly matters to each individual. I've adapted this framework specifically for real estate and retirement planning, helping my clients clarify their priorities so they can make confident, well-informed choices. When financial decisions are rooted in personal values, the path forward becomes clearer, and the stress of uncertainty fades. As we go through this exercise, I encourage you to think beyond the dollars and cents. What does financial security truly mean to you, and how can your real estate decisions support that vision?

How to Use the Values Ladder

1. Write the word *money* on a piece of paper.

2. Think about the first word or phrase that comes to mind when you ask yourself, "What's important about *money* to me?" People often start with things like *security or stability*, but your answer is unique to you.

3. Write down your answer above *money*. This is the first rung of your Values Ladder.

4. Now, ask yourself, "What's important about [*the previous answer*] to me?" Your answer might be *having more time with family or reducing stress*.

5.   Continue the process: "What's important about [*reducing stress*] to me?" The answer may lead to *pursuing passions or a sense of freedom.*

6.   Keep practicing this until you reach a deeper emotional value, such as *peace, love, or purpose.*

7.   If you are planning with a partner or spouse, each of you must complete your own Values Ladder. It's important to see and listen to "what's important about money" to each of you individually. There may be similarities, but they are never identical. Resist the urge to answer for one another.

At the end of this exercise, you will have built a Values Ladder, showing how each financial decision connects to your core values. The most powerful aspect of this tool is that it simplifies decision-making. If a financial choice does not align with your ladder, it's not the right choice—regardless of any perceived financial benefits.

Helpful Tip: It's not uncommon to feel stuck when trying to find a meaningful answer on the third or fourth rung of the values ladder. This is often the point where what matters most about money shifts from material concerns to social or emotional values, such as spending more time with family, pursuing passions, or prioritizing happiness. Sometimes, it can be helpful to ask yourself, "Who am I being?" or "What am I spending my time on?" Consider also, "Who would I like to be at this stage?"

Example Values Ladder:

Peace - *Who couldn't use a little more peace in their life*

Fulfillment - *leading to inner peace*

Pursuing passion - *Finding fulfillment in life*

Helping others - *Living a life pursuing passions*

Having more time with family - *Supporting and helping others*

Less stress - *Allowing more time for family*

Security - *Reducing stress and uncertainty*

Money - *A tool to achieve security*

Whenever you're faced with a difficult empirical decision—A, B, or C—simply test each option against the first rung of your Values Ladder. If it aligns, move up to the next rung and continue this process. If an option fails to align at any level, you'll know it doesn't support your fundamental values. If it does align all the way through, you can move forward with confidence, knowing you've made the best decision for yourself—regardless of the outcome.

A financial advisor's role is not necessarily to tell you what to do but to equip you with the information needed to make informed decisions that align with your values. The Values Ladder puts you in control, ensuring every financial move supports your personal priorities.

Beware the Dragon: Overcoming Emotional Barriers to Smart Decisions

But what happens when we don't follow our values? When financial decisions are made purely out of habit, fear, or the pressure to accumulate more? If we are not careful to practice values-based financial planning, we run the risk of something I call "Dragon Sickness." We've all seen movies or heard stories of the archetypal dragon—hoarding gold, obsessively guarding its treasure, blinded by greed, and ready to destroy anything that threatens its wealth. Well, this fantasy story plays out in real life all the time. This archetype exists for a reason: it serves as a warning about the dangers of prioritizing material wealth above all else.

When wealth accumulation becomes the sole focus, it can consume us, shaping our decisions in ways that may not align with what truly matters. It can lead to choices that hurt ourselves or others, all in the name of protecting and growing our assets.

When it comes to real estate and retirement, the goal shouldn't be just to hold onto real estate at all costs. Instead, the question should be: "Does this property still serve my values and my life?" If the answer is no, then it might be time to rethink your strategy.

*"If you don't know where you are going,
you'll end up someplace else."*
- Yogi Berra.

Chapter 2:

Real Estate Wealth 101

What is Your Home Really Worth?

Before making any major decisions about your home in retirement, it's crucial to fully understand its true financial value. Many homeowners are initially confused when they start considering their real estate as part of their retirement strategy, especially when it comes to distinguishing between market value and assessed value.

Market Value

Market value refers to the price your home would realistically sell for in the current market. This value is determined by various factors, including your property's location, condition, demand, interest rates, and the sale prices of comparable homes in the area. Essentially, the market value reflects what a buyer is willing to pay today. More importantly, it's the key figure that determines your ability to sell, leverage, or use your home's equity effectively in retirement planning.

Assessed Value

On the other hand, assessed value is the value assigned to your property by your municipality or province, primarily for tax purposes. While assessed value is used for property taxes, it often lags behind actual market conditions. In a rising market, your home's market value could be much higher than its assessed value—while in a downturn, the opposite could be true.

A clear example of the distinction between market value and assessed value can be seen in agricultural land zoning.

Properties classified as farms often have much lower assessed values, which in turn reduces property taxes, even if their market value is considerably higher due to factors like development potential or the land's desirability. For retirees holding onto farmland or large properties, understanding this difference is key. Your property taxes may be low, but the market value could mean it's a significant asset that requires careful planning for sale, transfer, or redevelopment.

If you're considering downsizing, selling, or leveraging your home's equity, understanding your home's market value is essential. A professional appraisal or a consultation with a real estate agent can give you a much clearer and more accurate picture than relying solely on the assessed value listed on your tax bill.

The Hidden Wealth in Your Property

There are three key areas to consider when evaluating your home as an asset, and we will delve deeper into each of these in later chapters:

Rental Income Potential

Many retirees sit on an untapped income source: their own home. Whether it's a legal suite, a short-term rental, or a portion of the property, renting part of your home can provide financial flexibility and supplement retirement income. For retirees, this can provide a steady stream of additional income. Short-term rentals, such as those through platforms like Airbnb, can also be a profitable option, depending on local regulations and zoning laws.

Land Value & Development Potential

In some regions, the land your home sits on may be worth more than the house itself. If the zoning laws allow, you might have the potential to subdivide the property, build a laneway house, or even redevelop the land entirely. A quick conversation with your municipality or a zoning expert can help you understand if your property has untapped development potential.

This could significantly increase the value of your property. To explore these potential options, it's helpful to have a conversation with a local commercial realtor who can assess the feasibility of these changes and help you understand the potential of your land.

Home Equity

Many homeowners view their home primarily as a place to live, not as a financial asset. However, the equity built up in your home can be accessed in various ways to provide cash flow during retirement. Options include downsizing, using a reverse mortgage, or taking out a Home Equity Line of Credit (HELOC). While these can provide valuable financial relief, it's essential to approach them with caution. Always consult with a trusted financial advisor before moving forward, as some services come with steep fees for setup or cancellation. Understanding the pros and cons of these options is critical to making informed decisions that align with your retirement goals.

Note: While accessing home equity can provide valuable liquidity, these strategies should be approached carefully. High fees, interest costs, and long-term financial implications should all be considered before borrowing against your home.

Capital Gains vs. Principal Residence Exemption

When you sell a property in Canada for more than you paid for it, the profit is called capital gain. Generally, 50% of that gain is taxable. However, if the property was your principal residence for every year you owned it, the Principal Residence Exemption allows you to avoid paying tax on that gain.

Vendor Take-Back Mortgage

A Vendor take-back (VTB) mortgage is a type of financing where the seller of a property also acts as a lender, allowing the buyer to borrow a portion of the purchase price directly from them. Instead of the buyer borrowing the full amount from a bank, the seller "takes back" a mortgage for part of the price, often to help the buyer qualify or to speed up a sale.

For example, if a home sells for $600,000 and the buyer can only get a bank mortgage for $500,000, the seller might agree to lend the remaining $100,000 themselves, secured against the property, just like a real mortgage. More on this in Chapter 9.

Common Psychological Biases That Lead to Costly Mistakes

Real estate decisions are deeply personal, often tied to emotions and long-held beliefs. However, psychological biases can cloud judgment, leading to suboptimal financial decisions. Recognizing these biases can help you make more rational choices when managing your home in retirement.

Here are six common biases to be aware of as you consider your options.

1. **Loss Aversion**: People feel the pain of losses more intensely than they feel the pleasure of equivalent gains. This can lead to overly conservative investing, selling too quickly after a market drop, or holding onto a declining asset too long in hopes of recovering losses.

2. **Confirmation Bias**: Investors tend to seek out and favour information that confirms their pre-existing beliefs while ignoring evidence that contradicts them. This can result in poor investment choices, such as sticking with a bad investment simply because it aligns with prior expectations.

3. **Overconfidence Bias**: Many investors believe they are better at making financial decisions than they actually are. This can lead to excessive trading, underestimating risk, or believing they can consistently time the market—usually resulting in lower returns.

4. **Recency Bias**: People give more weight to recent events than historical data. For example, if the market has been doing well, they may assume it will continue to rise indefinitely, leading to overexposure or risk. Conversely, after a downturn, they may become overly pessimistic and avoid investing altogether.

5. **Herd Mentality**: Investors often follow the crowd, buying assets when prices are high due to fear of missing out (FOMO) and selling in panic during downturns. This behaviour contributes to market bubbles and crashes.

6. **Cognitive Framing Bias**: This refers to the tendency for people to perceive and interpret financial decisions differently depending on how information is presented or "framed." This bias can lead individuals to make suboptimal choices by mentally categorizing assets in rigid ways rather than considering their full financial picture.

Many of my clients view their homes as untouchable rather than a financial tool. However, a $1 million home is a real asset. Whether through downsizing, renting, or strategic borrowing, it can provide greater financial security rather than simply remaining a dormant source of wealth.

RRSPs, RRIFs, TFSAs & Non-Registered Accounts: The Basics

Your home isn't the only financial asset that requires strategic planning in retirement. Your investment accounts—RRSPs, RRIFs, TFSAs, and non-registered funds—play a crucial role in generating income while minimizing taxes. Understanding how to withdraw from these accounts efficiently, in relation to your real estate, can play a key role in how to preserve wealth and support your retirement goals.

Registered Retirement Savings Plan (RRSP)

- Contributions are tax-deductible (reduce taxable income).
- Growth is tax-deferred until withdrawal.
- Must convert to an RRIF by age 71 and first mandatory withdrawal at age 72.
- Withdrawals are fully taxable as income.

Registered Retirement Income Fund (RRIF)

- Converts RRSP savings into a steady income stream.
- Mandatory minimum withdrawals start at age 72 and increase annually.
- Withdrawals are fully taxable as income.

Tax-Free Savings Account (TFSA)

- No tax on growth or withdrawals.
- Ideal for emergency funds or tax-free income.
- Use TFSAs for big purchases (travel, home renovations) without triggering tax.
- It can be used to offset excessive RRIF withdrawals to manage tax brackets.

- Use to withdraw income with lower tax impact than RRSPs/RRIFs.

Non-Registered Investment Accounts

- Tax will apply to growth; no tax on withdrawal of principal.
- No contribution limits, but subject to taxes on growth.
- Canadian Dividends receive preferential tax treatment.
- Use to withdraw income with a lower tax impact than RRSPs/RRIFs.

Understanding your home's market value, its income-generating potential, key biases to look out for, and your other retirement assets is the foundation for what lies ahead. In the following chapters, we'll dive deeper into specific strategies, explore real-life situations, and uncover tailored approaches that can make all the difference in your retirement journey. With each step, you'll gain practical insights to help you confidently navigate your unique path. The journey may begin here, but the possibilities are endless as we unlock the full potential of your real estate wealth together.

"The secret to getting ahead is getting started."

- Mark Twain.

Chapter 3:

Turning Home Equity into Opportunity

Home equity is often one of the largest untapped financial resources for homeowners. While many view their home purely as a place to live, it can also serve as a strategic financial tool. Whether through a Home Equity Line of Credit (HELOC), refinancing, or leveraging equity for investments, homeowners can optimize their wealth without necessarily selling their property. This chapter explores different ways to strategically use home equity while managing risks effectively.

How to Use a HELOC the Right Way

A HELOC is a revolving line of credit that allows homeowners to borrow against the equity they've built in their property. Unlike a traditional loan that provides a lump sum, a HELOC offers flexible access to funds up to a predetermined limit, similar to a credit card. Borrowers can draw from the HELOC as needed and repay it on their own schedule as long as they stay within the lender's terms.

The borrowing limit for a HELOC is usually based on a percentage of the home's appraised value, typically ranging from 65% to 80%, minus any outstanding mortgage balance. Since a HELOC is secured by the property, it generally comes with lower interest rates than unsecured loans or credit cards. However, most HELOCs have variable interest rates tied to the prime lending rate, meaning payments can fluctuate over time based on market conditions. While this can lead to cost savings when rates are low, it also introduces uncertainty in borrowing costs.

One of the biggest advantages of a HELOC is its flexibility. Borrowers can access funds whenever needed rather than taking out a fixed lump sum. The interest rates are usually lower than credit cards or personal loans, making it a cost-effective borrowing option. During the draw period, borrowers can make interest-only payments, which can improve cash flow management. A HELOC operates as reusable credit, meaning as funds are repaid, they become available to borrow again, offering long-term financial flexibility.

However, there are also risks to consider. Since a HELOC has a variable interest rate, payments have the potential to increase, which could lead to higher borrowing costs. The ease of access to funds can also lead to over-borrowing, creating unnecessary debt. While a HELOC provides financial flexibility, it's essential to avoid over-leveraging.

Additionally, if investments decline in value, homeowners may still owe the full borrowed amount, potentially leading to financial strain. Most importantly, because a HELOC is secured by the home, failure to make payments could result in foreclosure. If property values drop significantly or a borrower's financial situation changes, lenders may reduce or cancel the HELOC, limiting access to funds at a critical time.

The Situation: Mark and Lisa, both in their late 50s, live in Vancouver and have been steadily building their wealth. Their home, now worth $1.2 million, is mortgage-free, and they have a solid investment portfolio. While they're on track for retirement, they want to accelerate their wealth accumulation without disrupting their current cash flow or selling investments prematurely. They explore ways to leverage their home equity to invest strategically.

The Strategy: They decide to set up a HELOC for 33% for the homes equity or $400,000, allowing them to access their home equity while maintaining ownership. Instead of withdrawing for lifestyle expenses, they strategically invest a portion into a diversified portfolio, focusing on dividend-paying stocks and tax-efficient assets. The investment returns exceed the interest cost of the HELOC, and since the borrowed funds are used for investment purposes, the interest is tax-deductible.*

For non-registered investment accounts only.

The Outcome: Over time, their investments grow, generating additional income and long-term appreciation. The dividends help offset the HELOC interest costs, and they make structured repayments as their portfolio gains. By leveraging their home equity wisely, they accelerate their wealth-building strategy without tapping into their core retirement savings.

The Lesson: A HELOC can be a powerful tool for wealth creation when used strategically for investments rather than lifestyle expenses. Proper planning allows homeowners to enhance their financial position without selling their homes or disrupting their long-term investment strategy.

Refinancing Before Selling: When it Makes Sense

Refinancing before selling involves securing a new mortgage before listing the home for sale, often with better terms or a higher loan amount. This strategy can be useful in several situations. Homeowners looking to maximize their sale price may refinance to access their home equity and fund renovations that increase market value. Others who plan to purchase a new home before selling their current one may use refinancing as a form of bridge financing, ensuring they have the necessary liquidity to cover the transition. Additionally, refinancing can be a way to consolidate high-interest debt, allowing homeowners to use their home equity to pay off outstanding balances before moving. In some cases, refinancing may also help avoid costly prepayment penalties by switching lenders or restructuring the mortgage in a way that reduces fees. Even if a homeowner doesn't plan to sell immediately, securing better mortgage terms through refinancing can provide more financial flexibility if they decide to hold onto the home for a little longer.

One of the key advantages of refinancing before selling is the potential for a higher sale price. By using funds for strategic renovations or debt restructuring, homeowners can make their property more attractive to buyers, increasing its marketability. Refinancing can also help with financial positioning, ensuring liquidity for purchasing a new home before selling the old one. If mortgage rates have declined, refinancing can reduce carrying costs in the short term, making it more affordable to hold onto the property until a sale is completed.

However, there are also downsides to consider. Refinancing comes with added costs, including closing fees, legal expenses, and potential penalties, which may reduce financial gains from the sale. If the home does not sell quickly, homeowners may find themselves carrying a larger loan balance, which can create financial strain. Additionally, if the real estate market declines, refinancing at a higher loan amount could result in lower-than-expected net proceeds from the sale.

Refinancing before selling can be a valuable financial tool, but it requires careful planning to ensure that the benefits outweigh the risks. Homeowners should evaluate their market conditions, expected sale timeline, and overall financial goals before proceeding.

The Situation: Matt and Kathy, both in their early 60s, plan to downsize and move to a condo in Parksville. Their current home in Courtenay is worth $850,000 but needs updates before selling. They estimate that strategic renovations, including a kitchen upgrade, new flooring, and exterior work, will cost $75,000. These improvements are expected to increase their home's value by at least $125,000.

The Strategy: They refinance their mortgage, borrowing an extra $75,000 to fund the renovations. Since they plan to sell within a year, they negotiate a short-term fixed rate with minimal prepayment penalties.

The Outcome: The updated home sells within two weeks for $975,000, yielding a $125,000 increase over its pre-renovation value of $850,000. After paying off the refinanced mortgage, they walk away with a higher net profit, making their condo purchase much easier. They effectively used their home equity to invest in their own property and increase their return.

The Lesson: Refinancing before selling can be a smart move when used strategically to boost a home's market value and increase net proceeds.

Using Home Equity to Build an Investment Portfolio

For investors looking to optimize their wealth, borrowing against home equity to invest in a portfolio can be a strategic move—if done carefully. By using a HELOC, refinancing, or an investment loan, individuals can access capital to invest in a diversified portfolio of stocks, ETFs, or other assets. This strategy is most effective when market valuations are low, allowing investors to buy at a discount and benefit from long-term appreciation. However, the structure of the investment account matters, as it impacts both tax efficiency and cash flow management.

If funds are invested in an RRSP, the investor benefits from an immediate tax deduction, which can help offset some of the short-term interest costs of borrowing. This approach is particularly effective for high-income earners with unused

RRSP contribution room, as the tax refund can be reinvested or used to pay down debt. On the other hand, investing in a TFSA does not provide an immediate tax benefit but offers long-term, tax-free growth, making it ideal for assets with strong upside potential. Finally, if the borrowed funds are invested in a non-registered account, the interest on the loan may be tax deductible, provided the investments meet eligibility requirements (i.e., generating taxable income rather than just capital gains).

A well-structured approach to leveraged investing balances risk and reward while considering market conditions, cash flow needs, and tax implications. The following example illustrates how this strategy can be applied effectively during a market downturn.

The Situation: David, a 48-year-old professional, has accumulated significant home equity and has $60,000 in unused RRSP contribution room. With markets experiencing a downturn, he sees an opportunity to buy quality investments at discounted prices. However, his available cash flow is limited due to high taxation on his salary, and he is looking for a way to invest without disrupting his budget. After speaking with his financial advisor, David decides to use a HELOC to invest strategically, splitting his funds between his RRSP and TFSA to maximize both short- and long-term benefits.

The Strategy: David borrows $75,000 from his HELOC at an interest rate of 6%. To reduce his taxable income for the year, he contributes $50,000 to his RRSP, generating a $22,000 tax refund based on his marginal tax rate. He then uses part of this refund to cover the first year of interest payments on his HELOC, reducing the immediate financial burden of the loan. The remaining $25,000 is invested in his TFSA, allowing for long-term, tax-free growth.

By structuring his investment this way, David benefits from:

- A large tax refund, which offsets borrowing costs in the short term.
- Tax-free growth in his TFSA, where gains will never be taxed.
- Long-term compounding in both accounts, taking advantage of lower market valuations.

The Outcome: Over the next five years, the market recovers, and David's portfolio grows at an average annual return of 8%. His $50,000 RRSP investment grows to $74,000, and his $25,000 TFSA investment grows to $37,000. Meanwhile, he steadily pays down his HELOC using a combination of his tax savings and regular income. By year five, his portfolio value has increased significantly, and his HELOC is nearly paid off. If he had waited to invest using only his savings, he would have missed out on both the market rebound and the compounding growth on a larger initial investment.

The Lesson: Borrowing to invest can be a powerful wealth-building strategy when executed with a clear plan. By leveraging home equity during a market downturn, David was able to invest at a discount and amplify long-term growth. The key to success was structuring the investment to take advantage of tax efficiency—using the RRSP for an immediate tax refund and the TFSA for future tax-free gains. However, leveraged investing is not without risks. It requires careful management of debt, a long-term mindset, and the ability to maintain the loan during market volatility. Investors considering this strategy should ensure they have a stable cash flow and a solid risk management plan before proceeding.

Should you Invest in Rental Properties?

Using home equity to invest in rental properties is a common strategy for growing a real estate portfolio without requiring a large upfront cash investment. A HELOC allows homeowners to borrow against their home's equity, providing flexible access to funds for a down payment, renovations, or other property-related expenses. Alternatively, a second mortgage enables homeowners to take out an additional loan against their property, which can be used to finance the purchase of a rental property. Both options offer a way to expand real estate holdings, and come with distinct risks and rewards.

One of the primary advantages of leveraging home equity is the potential for higher returns. By using existing equity instead of personal savings, investors can acquire rental properties with minimal upfront capital, maximizing long-term gains. If the rental property is cash-flow positive, rental income can help cover the loan payments, reducing the financial burden. Additionally, interest on borrowed funds used for rental investments is often tax-deductible, improving overall tax efficiency. Investing in real estate also provides an opportunity to diversify assets, reducing reliance on stock markets, pensions, or other traditional investments.

However, using home equity for rental investments carries risks. A downturn in the rental market or unexpected expenses could make it challenging to cover loan payments, increasing financial strain. Interest rates may rise, increasing carrying costs on both the primary residence and the rental property. Additionally, lenders assess whether an investor can afford to carry debt on both properties, which may make it harder to qualify for a mortgage. Committing a large portion of home equity to a rental property can limit financial flexibility, making it harder to access funds for emergencies or retirement. Rental properties are only profitable if they remain occupied. If tenants leave unexpectedly or market demand shifts, investors must have financial reserves to cover mortgage payments and expenses during vacant periods. Lastly, while leverage amplifies gains in strong markets, it can exaggerate losses in downturns, leaving investors with higher debt and potentially reduced property values.

Carefully evaluating these factors is crucial before using home equity to invest in rental properties. A well-planned approach considers cash flow, interest rates, market conditions, and long-term investment goals to ensure that leverage remains a tool for growth rather than a financial burden.

The Situation: Jennifer and Barry, both in their late 50s, own a mortgage-free home in Nanaimo worth $1.2 million. As they plan for retirement, they are looking for additional income sources beyond their pensions and RRSPs.

The Strategy: Jennifer and Barry decide to take out a $250,000 HELOC against their home, using $150,000 as a down payment on a $600,000 rental duplex and setting aside $100,000 for renovations and contingencies. The duplex generates $4,500 per month in rental income, while their HELOC payments amount to $1,500 per month on an interest-only basis at a 7% rate.

The Outcome: After accounting for property taxes (approximately $375 per month), maintenance costs (about $500 per month based on the 1% rule), and mortgage payments (estimated at $3,000 per month based on a 25-year amortization at 5% interest), they still generate $1,200 per month in positive cash flow. As the property appreciates over time, their overall net worth increases. In 15 years, they plan to sell or refinance the rental to help fund their retirement.

The Lesson: By strategically leveraging their home equity, Jennifer and Barry built a new income stream without selling assets or depleting their savings.

"Opportunities multiply as they are seized."

- Sun Tzu.

Chapter 4:

Tax Deductible Mortgage Strategy

The Smith Maneuver: Using Your Mortgage to Build Wealth

The Smith Maneuver is ideal for homeowners in their peak earning years, with a stable income, who are looking for long-term wealth accumulation strategies to offset taxes.

Unlike in the U.S., mortgage interest on a personal residence in Canada is not tax-deductible. However, the Smith Maneuver offers a way to convert non-deductible mortgage debt into tax-deductible investment debt, helping homeowners reduce their tax burden while building an investment portfolio.

This leveraged investment strategy involves using a readvanceable mortgage—a combination of a mortgage and a HELOC—to borrow against your home's equity and invest the borrowed funds.

The Smith Maneuver is a powerful wealth-building strategy, but it requires discipline, financial stability, and a long-term mindset. Before implementing this strategy, it's essential to consult a financial advisor to ensure it aligns with your overall retirement and investment plan.

The simplest way of understanding how the Smith Maneuver works is the following five step process that you repeat until the mortgage is paid off:

Step 1: Setting Up the Readvanceable Mortgage

Step 2: Paying Down the Mortgage and Accessing the HELOC

Step 3: Using the Borrowed Funds to Invest

Step 4: Claiming Tax Deductions

Step 5: Reinvesting Tax Savings for Compound Growth

The Smith Maneuver is best suited for homeowners with a stable income and reliable cash flow, ensuring they can comfortably manage both their mortgage and HELOC payments. It is particularly beneficial for long-term investors who can commit to a 10+ year horizon, giving their investments time to grow and weather market fluctuations. This strategy also requires a high risk tolerance, making it a good fit for those who are comfortable with both debt and investing.

However, the Smith Maneuver may not be ideal for everyone. Those nearing retirement or with a low risk tolerance may find the strategy too volatile for their financial needs. Homeowners who prefer to remain debt-free may be uncomfortable with the borrowing aspect of the strategy. Anyone who may need to sell their home in the near future could face disruptions as the strategy relies on long-term participation to be effective.

Risks

For the Smith Maneuver to be successful, investment returns must outpace the cost of borrowing over time. If HELOC interest rates rise, borrowing costs will increase, which can reduce overall profitability. This risk is particularly relevant for those investing in fixed-rate assets like bonds, as their returns may not be high enough to offset rising HELOC expenses. Investing in stocks or real estate carries inherent market risks. If values decline, the borrowed money could lose value, leading to potential losses if forced to sell.

Tax Deductibility Rules

The CRA only allows interest deductions on money borrowed for investments that generate income, such as dividend-paying stocks or rental properties. Borrowing to invest in RRSPs or TFSAs does not qualify for a tax deduction, making it important to structure the strategy correctly to maximize benefits.

The Situation: Jonah and Sarah are a married couple living in Toronto. They recently purchased a home for $800,000 with a $600,000 mortgage. They have solid incomes and want to accelerate their wealth-building while reducing taxes.

The Strategy:

Step 1: Setting Up the Readvanceable Mortgage

- Their mortgage lender offers a readvanceable mortgage with a HELOC component.

- Each month, as they make principal payments, their HELOC limit increases by the principal portion amount.

Step 2: Using the Smith Maneuver

- Each month, they pay $3,000 toward their mortgage: $2,000 goes to interest, and $1,000 goes to principal.

- Their HELOC limit increases by $1,000 after every payment.

- They borrow that $1,000 and invest it in an eligible investment, such as a Canadian dividend-paying ETF.

Step 3: Growing Investments & Tax Deductions

- Over a year, they borrow and invest $12,000 at a 5% interest rate.

- Assuming an investment of $1,000 per month into a Canadian Dividend ETF that had an average annual growth of 3% and an annual 4% dividend yield, they earn approximately $196 in capital appreciation and approximately $330 in dividends in the first year.

- They claim the HELOC interest of roughly $330 for the first year as a tax deduction, reducing their taxable income and getting an annual refund of $208 (based on a 40% tax bracket) in their first year.

Step 4: Compounding Wealth Over 20 Years

- After 20 years, assuming a 7% annual return, their investment portfolio grows to $500,000+.

- Meanwhile, their original mortgage is either close to or fully paid off, depending on whether tax refunds are used against the principle of the mortgage.

- They continue using the HELOC to invest and generate tax-efficient income.

The Outcome: Cash flow from dividends helped offset borrowing costs, while the mortgage had additional payment applied using the tax refunds and a large investment portfolio was built. This strategy led to significant tax savings over 20 years.

The Lesson: Jonah and Sarah's case highlights the power of leveraging a readvanceable mortgage to accelerate wealth-building while reducing taxes. By using their monthly mortgage payments to increase their HELOC limit and investing those funds in dividend-paying assets, they were able to generate passive income, offset borrowing costs, and enjoy tax deductions.

Over time, this strategy not only paid off their mortgage but also built a substantial investment portfolio, demonstrating the long-term benefits of disciplined investing and tax-efficient financial strategies.

Leveraged investing strategies, including the Smith Maneuver, carry significant risk and are not suitable for all investors. These strategies should only be considered with the guidance of a qualified professional, who understands your full financial picture.

"Don't let the tax tail wag the dog."

- Author unknown.

Chapter 5:

Real Estate Income & Taxes - What You Need to Know

Misunderstanding how real estate income and sales are taxed in Canada can lead to unexpected tax bills, missed deductions, or even costly penalties. Whether you're renting out a basement suite, running an Airbnb, or selling a property, the tax treatment varies significantly. This chapter provides a high-level overview of the tax implications of various real estate activities, including renting to family, short-term vs long-term rental income, homestay or exchange student income, and selling a principal residence vs selling secondary property such as a cottage. It covers other key tax considerations, such as HST/GST and allowable deductions.*

This is not to be considered tax advice, and all tax-related questions must be confirmed with your tax professional.

Short-Term Rental: How It's Taxed

- Rental income earned from short-term stays (less than 30 days) is considered business income and must be reported on your tax return.

- If you provide additional services (e.g., meals, cleaning, concierge), the CRA may classify it as a business rather than a rental income.

- GST/HST may apply if gross rental income exceeds $30,000 per year.

- Expenses like mortgage interest, property taxes, utilities, and maintenance can be deducted to reduce taxable income.

Case Study: Airbnb Host in Victoria

The Situation: Sarah owns a condo in downtown Victoria, BC, which she rents out on Airbnb for $250 per night, generating $45,000 in annual revenue.

The Outcome: Sarah is required to report her rental income on her tax return. As her earnings exceed the $30,000 GST/HST threshold, she must collect and remit GST on her bookings. She deducts eligible expenses such as mortgage interest, strata fees, cleaning, and repairs, reducing her taxable income to $18,000. To manage her tax obligations effectively, Sarah sets aside 30% of her net income in savings.

The Lesson: Airbnb hosts must track expenses carefully and understand when GST/HST applies.

Long-Term Rental: How It's Taxed

- Rental income from long-term tenants (leases of 30+ days) is considered passive rental income and is fully taxable.

- Owners can deduct expenses such as mortgage interest, property taxes, insurance, maintenance, and property management fees.

- Capital Cost Allowance (CCA) can be used to defer taxes by depreciating the property's value over time (but may trigger taxes when selling).

Capital Cost Allowance (CCA) is the depreciation that landlords in Canada can claim on rental properties to account for wear and tear over time. It allows property owners to deduct a portion of the property's cost from their rental income, reducing taxable income. However, CCA cannot be used to create or increase a rental loss, and when the property is sold, previously claimed CCA may be subject to recapture, meaning it gets added back to taxable income.

Case Study: Retired Couple with a Rental Property

The Situation: Kelly and Susan rent out a townhouse for $2,500 per month, generating $30,000 per year in rental income.

The Outcome: After deducting $15,000 in expenses (property taxes, insurance, maintenance, utilities, and property management fees) their taxable rental income is $15,000. They choose not to claim CCA, avoiding a large tax bill when they sell the property later.

The Lesson: Long-term rental income is fully taxable, but deductions help reduce the tax burden.

Homestay & Exchange Student Income: How It's Taxed

- Income earned from hosting an international student or homestay guest is taxable.

- If a host provides food, laundry, or other services, the CRA may classify the income as business income rather than rental income.

- Tax-Free Exception: If hosting through a non-profit organization, some or all the income may be tax-exempt.

- Expenses related to hosting (extra utilities, groceries, wear-and-tear) may be deductible.

Case Study: Hosting a Student in Nanaimo

The Situation: Marlow and Lela rent out a furnished basement suite in Nanaimo, BC, to an international student for $1,200 per month, including the room, meals, and transportation.

The Outcome: They report $14,400 in taxable income for the year. To offset some of the earnings, they deduct $5,000 in related expenses, which include additional utilities, groceries, household supplies, minor home repairs, and a portion of their home insurance. These deductions lower their taxable amount to $9,400. They confirm with the program that no portion of the income qualifies for a tax exemption.

The Lesson: Exchange student income is usually taxable. It is essential to determine in advance which expenses qualify as deductions and whether any exemptions apply when hosting through registered programs.

Selling your Principal Residence: How It's Taxed

- The Principal Residence Exemption (PRE) allows homeowners to sell their home tax-free if it has been their primary residence for every year they owned it.

- If a property was rented out for part of the time, only a portion of the gain is exempt.

- Homeowners must now report the sale on their tax return, even if no tax is owed.

Case Study: Downsizing with No Tax Bill

The Situation: After 20 years in their Vancouver home, Peter and Linda sell for $1.5 million, having originally bought it for $400,000.

The Outcome: Since it was their principal residence the entire time, the $1.1 million capital gain ($1.5 million sale price minus the original purchase price of $400,000) is fully tax-exempt. They still report the sale on their tax return.

The Lesson: The Principal Residence Exemption eliminates taxes on capital gains for most homeowners.

Selling a Rental or Secondary Property: How It's Taxed

- Unlike a primary home, selling a rental or secondary property triggers capital gains tax.

- Capital gains tax: 50% of the capital gain is taxable at your marginal tax rate.

- Selling costs (legal fees, realtor commissions) and capital improvements (renovations, not maintenance) can reduce the taxable gain.

Case Study: Selling a Cottage

The Situation: Emma sells her family vacation cottage for $800,000, which she inherited at a fair market value of $400,000. She has documented $50,000 in past renovations.

The Outcome: The capital gain is $400,000, but only $200,000 (50%) is taxable. With a 35% tax rate, she owes $70,000 in taxes. Due to documents verifying $50,000 in past renovations, her taxable gain is reduced, saving her $8,750 in taxes.

The Lesson: Keeping records of renovation costs helps reduce capital gains tax when selling a rental or secondary property.

Renting to Family: Smart or Risky?

Many Canadian retirees own rental properties, and some choose to rent them to family members at below-market rates. While this may seem like a generous or practical arrangement, there are important tax considerations that can impact how the property is treated for tax purposes—especially when it comes to capital gains.

Capital Gains Tax Still Applies

If you sell the property in the future, any increase in value from the time you acquired it to the time you sold it is subject to capital gains tax, just like a regular rental property.

Below-Market Rent Can Disqualify Deductible Expenses

If you charge less than fair market rent, the Canada Revenue Agency (CRA) may classify it as a "cost-sharing" arrangement rather than a true rental business. This means you can't claim rental expenses (such as mortgage interest, property tax, and maintenance) to offset rental income.

Principal Residence Exemption May Not Apply

If you live in a part of the property while renting to your family, only the portion you personally occupy may qualify for the principal residence exemption, reducing capital gains tax. The rented portion may be subject to capital gains when sold.

Deemed Disposition Risk

If you later decide to give the property to a family member instead of selling it at fair market value, the CRA treats it as if you sold it at market value, triggering potential capital gains tax even if no money is exchanged.

Case Study: The Hidden Tax Cost of Renting to Family

The Situation: David, 68, owns a rental condo in Victoria, BC, that he originally purchased for $400,000. Five years ago, he decided to rent the property to his son, James, for $1,000 per month. This is significantly below the fair market rent of $2,500 per month.

The Outcome: Because David rented below market value, the CRA classified the arrangement as a cost-sharing agreement, denying him deductions for property tax, mortgage interest, and condo fees.

Now, at age 73, David decides to sell the condo for $700,000. Since the property was an investment, he must report a capital gain of $300,000 ($700,000 - $400,000). With 50% of the gain taxable, $150,000 is added to his income for that year. If his marginal tax rate is 40%, he faces a tax bill of $60,000 on the sale.

Alternative Scenario: If David instead sells the condo to his son James for $500,000—below market value—the CRA still considers the sale at fair market value ($700,000) for tax purposes. This means that although David only received $500,000 from the sales, he still owes capital gains tax on $300,000.

The Lesson: Renting to family at below-market rates may seem like a simple and generous decision, but it can lead to unexpected tax consequences, including denied deductions and significant capital gains taxes upon sale. It's essential to plan ahead and consult a professional to ensure tax efficiency while helping family members.

Other Tax Considerations

When converting a principal residence into a rental property—or vice versa—the CRA may apply change in use rules, treating the transition as a "deemed disposition" that could trigger capital gains tax (read more about deemed dispositions in Chapter 10). For those who frequently buy and sell properties, the CRA's flipping tax rules may come into play, classifying profits as fully taxable business income rather than capital gains. Similarly, selling a pre-construction condo before taking ownership, known as a pre-sale assignment, is also considered business income and is fully taxable rather than benefiting from the lower capital gains tax rate. Understanding these tax implications is crucial for avoiding unexpected liabilities.

Tax laws are complex and subject to change. Always consult a qualified tax professional before making decisions based on the information in this chapter.

Real Estate & Taxation Summary Chart

Type of Income/ Transaction	How It's Taxed	Key Deductions Available	Additional Notes
Short-Term Rental (Airbnb, VRBO, etc.)	Fully taxable as rental or business income. GST/HST applies if income exceeds $30,000/year.	Mortgage interest, property taxes, utilities, maintenance, cleaning, platform fees, insurance.	GST/HST registration may be required. Additional services (e.g., meals, tours) may classify as business income.
Homestay / Exchange Student Income	Fully taxable as rental or business income unless tax-exempt under a registered program. GST/HST may apply.	Utilities, groceries (portion related to hosting), maintenance.	GST/HST registration may be required. Some non-profit school programs offer tax-free allowances (check with the program).
Long-Term Rental Income	Fully taxable as passive rental income. GST/HST exempt.	Mortgage interest, property taxes, insurance, maintenance, property management fees, utilities (if included in rent).	Capital Cost Allowance (CCA) can defer taxes but may lead to recapture tax when selling.

Type of Income/ Transaction	How It's Taxed	Key Deductions Available	Additional Notes
Sale of a Principal Residence	Tax-free if the home was your principal residence for every year owned.	N/A.	Must report the sale on your tax return, even if no tax is owed. If part of the home was rented, partial exemption might apply.
Sale of a Rental or Secondary Property (e.g., Cottage)	Capital gains tax applies: 50% of the gain is taxable at your marginal rate.	Selling costs (legal fees, realtor commission), capital improvements (not maintenance).	If converted from a principal residence to a rental, a deemed disposition rule may apply.
Flipping or Pre-Sale Assignment Sales	Fully taxable as business income (not capital gains). No 50% exemption. GST/HST may apply.	Selling costs.	GST/HST registration may be required. The CRA may audit frequent property sales and classify them as business activity.
Multi-Unit House Hacking (Owner-Occupied Rental)	Fully taxable as personal income.	Same as rental properties (for the rented portion).	Can still qualify for principal residence exemption on the owner's portion.

Stage 2:

During Retirement - Simplify, Optimize, and Create Cash Flow

A few years ago, I sat down with a couple in their late 60s who had worked hard their entire lives and done relatively well financially. But they were facing a common problem. Their assets were spread across multiple banks, their rental property required constant upkeep, and they didn't have a clear understanding of how all these moving parts worked together to provide them with reliable cash flow. They knew they should be in a good position, but they felt stuck—frustrated by the lack of organization and unsure how to transition from simply accumulating wealth to actually using it efficiently in retirement.

This is not uncommon. Life gets busy, and for years, we focus on growing our wealth. Then, seemingly overnight, the conversation shifts. Suddenly, it's no longer just about making more money, but ensuring income certainty and protecting what you've built. That transition can feel overwhelming, or scary, especially when there's no clear strategy in place.

I remember feeling a similar sense of uncertainty when I sold my first business, a home maintenance company. For years, I had poured my energy into growing the business, acquiring equipment, taking on new clients, and expanding operations. But when the time came to sell, I realized I had spent so much time building that I hadn't given much thought to how I'd extract value from it. What was the best way to structure the sale? How could I minimize taxes? And most importantly, how could I make sure the wealth I had created worked for me in the long run? The experience taught me an important lesson—accumulation is just one piece of the puzzle. Knowing how to transition from growth to sustainable income is just as critical.

In this section, we'll cover the key levers you can pull to make that transition smooth and effective. We'll rethink the role of real estate in retirement and explore how it can be a powerful tool for generating reliable income, extending the longevity of your assets, and creating peace of mind beyond traditional income sources.

"Beware of little expenses;
a small leak will sink a great ship."
- Benjamin Franklin.

Chapter 6:

The Real Cost of Keeping a Home in Retirement

Many retirees assume that staying in their house is the most cost-effective choice. However, homeownership comes with ongoing costs that can increase over time—especially as maintenance needs grow, property taxes rise, and insurance rates change.

This chapter explores the financial reality of keeping a home in retirement, helping you determine whether staying put is a sustainable and desirable choice.

The True Price of Maintenance, Property Taxes, and Insurance

Maintenance Costs

Even mortgage-free homes have significant carrying costs, which should be factored into long-term retirement planning. A general rule of thumb for home maintenance is to budget 1% of the property's value per year. For example, if your property is worth $900,000, this would be $9,000. This covers routine upkeep such as roofing, plumbing, electrical work, landscaping, and small repairs. Homeowners must account for property taxes and insurance, and those in strata properties should also budget for strata/HOA fees and potential special assessments.

Certain properties may have different costs:

Detached Homes: Higher maintenance costs, including roof replacement, driveway repairs, and exterior upkeep.

Condos & Townhomes: Maintenance is largely covered by strata/HOA fees, but special assessments can arise.

Older Homes: Higher maintenance costs due to aging infrastructure.

Example 1: Single-Family Home in Victoria ($1M value)

Expense	Estimated Annual Cost
Maintenance (1% rule)	$10,000
Property Tax (0.5-1.2% of value)	$6,000 - $12,000
Home Insurance	$2,500 - $4,500
Total Annual Cost	$18,500 - $26,500

Example 2: Condo in Nanaimo ($600K value, $450/month strata fee)

Expense	Estimated Annual Cost
Maintenance (Covered by strata)	Included in fees
Property Tax (0.5-1.2%)	$3,000 - $7,200
Home Insurance (Unit-specific)	$800 - $1,500
Strata Fees	$5,400
Total Annual Cost	$9,200 - $14,100

When Is Your Home Too Much to Handle?

Your home should support your lifestyle, not add stress or financial strain. If maintaining it becomes overwhelming, it may be time to consider downsizing or simplifying. Four key indicators can signal that change is needed.

If daily upkeep like yard work, snow shovelling, or cleaning gutters starts to feel like a burden, your home may no longer suit your lifestyle. Travelling more and using your home less often could make downsizing a practical choice, offering greater flexibility and freeing up time and resources for other interests. As mobility challenges arise, navigating a multi-story home can become increasingly difficult. Health conditions may create a need for single-level living or a community with support services, making it important to reassess whether your current home still meets your needs.

Beyond physical limitations, changes in personal preference can also indicate that it's time for a transition. A once lively home can start to feel empty after children move out, leading to a reconsideration of how much space is truly necessary. Extra bedrooms, once filled with the energy of a growing family, now sit unused, collecting dust. The desire to be closer to family or healthcare may outweigh sentimental attachments, while the rising costs of maintaining an aging property can turn what once felt like an investment into a financial and emotional burden.

Recognizing these signs can help you make a proactive decision about your home, ensuring it continues to enhance your quality of life rather than detract from it.

The Cost of Holding Onto "Too Much House"

Holding onto more space than you need comes with both financial and practical costs. Higher utility bills, property taxes, and maintenance expenses can drain retirement savings, while the time and effort required for upkeep may take away from the activities you truly enjoy.

Downsizing has the potential to save money and create a home that enhances your retirement years. A space that requires less effort and expense allows for greater freedom, whether that means travelling more, pursuing hobbies, or simply enjoying a stress-free living environment.

Budgeting for Aging in Place: Renovations & Accessibility Upgrades

Aging in place requires financial planning, but proactive renovations can help maintain independence. If you decide to stay in your home, modifying it for aging in place can be a smart investment. Here are some common renovations and estimated costs:

Upgrade	Estimated Cost
Stair Lift (Straight Staircase)	$3,000 - $5,000
Stair Lift (Curved Staircase)	$10,000 - $15,000
Walk-in Bathtub	$5,000 - $10,000
Grab Bars and Railings	$200 - $1,000
Wider Doorways for Wheelchair Access	$1,500 - $3,000 per door

Safety & Convenience Features

Upgrade	Estimated Cost
Smart Home Security System	$500 - $2,500
Automatic Lighting / Motion Sensors	$200 - $1,000
Lever Door Handles (Easier to Use than Knobs)	$40 - $150 per door

Secondary Bedroom for In-Home Help

If you plan to hire live-in assistance, you may need to renovate or repurpose a space in your home. Converting a basement or additional room into a private suite could cost between $20,000 and $50,000, depending on the extent of the work. Alternatively, converting a bedroom into a space for a caregiver could cost between $5,000 and $15,000, making it a more affordable option for those seeking less extensive changes.

Government Assistance for Home Modifications

There are several government programs available to help with the cost of home modifications. In British Columbia, the Home Renovation Tax Credit for Seniors provides a tax credit for eligible home modifications. The Canada Mortgage and Housing Corporation (CMHC) offers grants for accessibility modifications, helping homeowners make their homes safer and more accessible.

Reverse Mortgages: A Smart Solution or Last Resort?

A reverse mortgage allows homeowners aged 55 and older to access a portion of their home equity as tax-free cash while continuing to live in their home. Unlike a traditional mortgage, there are no required monthly payments. The loan is repaid when the homeowner sells the property, moves out, or passes away. The amount that can be borrowed is based on factors such as the homeowner's age and the property's appraised value, with most lenders allowing up to 55% of the home's value.

Borrowers can receive the funds as a lump sum, scheduled payments, or a combination of both, depending on their financial needs. However, interest accrues over time, increasing the total loan balance. While this strategy provides financial flexibility for retirees, it also reduces the remaining home equity available for heirs.

The Situation: Margaret, 78, lives alone in Nanaimo. She has no mortgage, and her home is valued at $900,000. Her children live out of province, and she prefers to remain in her home rather than move into assisted living. However, she needs extra funds to cover home care and accessibility modifications.

The Strategy: Margaret takes out a reverse mortgage for $300,000, structured as an initial $50,000 lump sum for renovations and then $2,000 per month for care services. She does not need to make monthly payments, allowing her to stay in her home comfortably for roughly another ten years before the loan is used up. At the same time if her home appreciates at 6% a year her home value would then be about 1.61 million.

The Outcome: She gets the home care she needs without draining her savings or asking her children for financial support. Her home continues to appreciate, offsetting some of the accruing loan interest. Her estate will settle the loan balance after she passes or moves out, ensuring she has financial stability in her later years.

The Lesson: Reverse mortgages can be a viable option for aging homeowners who want to access home equity while remaining independent.

"Wealth consists not in having great possessions, but in having few wants."

- Epictetus.

Chapter 7:

Should You Downsize?

For many retirees, the question of downsizing is an emotional one. Your home represents security, comfort, and memories, but it's also a major financial asset that can impact your retirement lifestyle, cash flow, and long-term stability. In this chapter, we'll explore the benefits, challenges, and alternative options to help you decide whether downsizing is the right move for you.

The Financial and Lifestyle Benefits of Downsizing: Freeing Up Cash & Reducing Expenses

One of the biggest advantages of downsizing is that it reduces your financial burden while increasing your flexibility. By moving to a smaller, more manageable home or even a different location, you can free up capital, lower expenses, and create a retirement plan with more options and more security.

Owning a large home often means that a significant portion of your wealth is tied up in an illiquid asset. By selling and downsizing to a smaller, more affordable home, you can free up cash and achieve a financial windfall. This shift can allow you to increase retirement savings or investment income, eliminate or reduce mortgage payments, and lower property taxes, insurance, and maintenance costs. Additionally, reducing utility bills and general upkeep expenses can further decrease your monthly financial obligations. The impact of these changes compounds over time. By spending less each year, you need less savings to maintain your lifestyle.

The Rule of 20 & 25: How Much Money Do You Really Need?

A general guideline for retirement income planning is the "Rule of 20" or "Rule of 25", which suggests that for every $1 you need to spend annually above your regular pension income sources in retirement, you need $20 - $25 saved and invested to generate that income for the rest of your life without running out. This figure comes from the Monte Carlo Simulation, which is a mathematical technique used to model uncertainty and risk against possible outcomes.

For example, if your home costs you $10,000 per year in taxes, maintenance, and utilities, you would need $200,000 to $250,000 in savings to cover those costs indefinitely. If downsizing reduces those costs to $5,000 per year, you now only need $100,000 to $125,000 in savings—a massive reduction in required retirement assets.

By lowering your cost of living, you significantly reduce financial pressure and increase flexibility in how you spend your income on things that are truly aligned with your values.

The Emotional Challenge of Leaving Your Home

The emotional side of downsizing can't be overlooked. Your home is a space filled with memories, familiarity, and a sense of stability. For many, letting go of your home feels like letting go of part of your identity.

But there's also a deeper, often unspoken transition happening during this stage of life. As we move from the wealth accumulation phase into retirement, there's a fundamental shift in mindset. For decades, your focus has likely been on building, growing, and maximizing. Retirement marks a new chapter where the priorities shift toward security, simplicity, and making your wealth work for you.

It's common to feel unsettled in this transition. Questions about purpose, value, and control often arise. While you're reallocating assets and adjusting budgets, you're also reshaping your mental image of who you are in this next stage of life. That's why decisions like downsizing or adjusting your real estate holdings can be so difficult. They're intertwined with emotion, identity, and the need for certainty.

Understanding and acknowledging this emotional layer is just as important as the financial analysis. That's why we take a values-based approach to retirement planning, so that both your numbers and your mindset are aligned. This will give you the peace of mind to move forward confidently.

One way to approach this transition is to separate a house as an asset from a home as a feeling. Your sense of security and comfort doesn't have to be tied to a specific property. It can move with you.

Here are a few ways to help with the emotional transition:

1. **Reflect on what truly makes your home "home."** Is it the physical space or the people, routines, and lifestyle it enables?

2. **Acknowledge the benefits of change.** A smaller home can still be comfortable while being easier to manage and freeing up time and energy for the things you love.

3. **Create a moving-forward mindset.** Downsizing doesn't mean losing your home; it means choosing a new space that better serves your retirement lifestyle.

Downsizing Pitfalls & How to Avoid Them

One major downside of downsizing is the potential loss of a valuable asset in the Canadian real estate market, which has historically outpaced inflation. While selling your home may free up cash in the short term, holding onto property can provide long-term financial growth and appreciation.

Additionally, downsizing can come with unexpected costs. You may need to invest in renovations or updates to make the new home more suitable for your needs. There could also be additional expenses such as hiring movers and managing the logistics of relocating.

Another consideration is the emotional toll of leaving a long-time home. For many, downsizing means leaving behind cherished memories, a familiar neighbourhood, and a sense of stability. This emotional aspect can be difficult to navigate, especially if the move is driven by necessity rather than choice.

Finally, while a smaller home may have lower maintenance costs, you'll still need to consider ongoing expenses such as property taxes, utilities, and insurance. In some cases, downsizing may not result in as significant savings as expected, especially if the market value of your new home is still high.

Before making a decision, it's important to weigh these potential downsides against the benefits of freeing up cash and simplifying your living situation.

"Someone is sitting in the shade today because someone planted a tree a long time ago."
- Warren Buffett.

Chapter 8:

Turning Wealth into Reliable Income

Retirement planning involves turning assets into a reliable income stream while maintaining financial security and peace of mind. In this chapter, we'll explore how to transition from saving to spending, covering market trends, structured income strategies, and tax-efficient account withdrawals.

Selling at The Right Time: When Should You Cash Out?

Many retirees worry about timing the market, hoping to sell at the "right moment." While short- and medium-term debt cycles exist (typically with interest rates rising and falling over 3 to 6 years) the best time to sell is when the numbers align with your retirement plans. Rather than chasing market highs, focus on whether selling supports your income needs, tax strategy, and long-term goals. Key factors to consider include:

- Cash flow: Do you need capital now, or can you wait?

- Market conditions: Predicting the absolute peak is unrealistic.

- Minimizing the liability of tax implications. Check out the Gap Year Strategy in the next chapter for an example.

- Ensuring that selling now will provide financial security without jeopardizing your future retirement plans.

The Six Steps to a Secure Retirement Income Plan

Much of the framework that we use to help our clients create a smooth transition from wealth accumulation to reliable retirement income is inspired by the work of Darryl Diamond, a leading financial advisor, educator, and speaker in Canada. His book, Retirement Income Blueprint, provides a comprehensive and in-depth guide to structuring retirement income in a way that maximizes security and flexibility. If you're looking for a deeper dive into this topic, I highly recommend his book as an excellent resource. In the meantime, this section will cover the key takeaways—particularly the importance of the cash wedge strategy and a structured six-step approach—to help ensure you have a steady and dependable income throughout retirement.

Step 1: Assess Your Life Stage

- Are you already retired or within a few years of retirement?
- What are your expected expenses (housing, travel, healthcare, etc.)?
- Do you plan to downsize or relocate?

Step 2: Define Your Retirement Income Goals

- How much after-tax income do you need per year?
- Do you have large one-time expenses coming up (e.g., home renovations, travel, helping family)?
- Will your spending be higher early in retirement and taper off later?

Step 3: Identify Income Sources

- Guaranteed Income: CPP, OAS, workplace pensions.

- Investment Income: RRIFs, TFSAs, rental properties.

- Other Sources: Part-time work, inheritance, home equity.

Step 4: Structure Your Income for Stability

- Layering Income Streams: Combining guaranteed and investment-based income.

- Setting Up a GIC (Guaranteed Income Certificate) ladder (Cash Wedge): Keeping 3 - 4 years of expenses in safe-laddered GIC investments.

- Withdrawing from accounts in a tax-efficient way.

Step 5: Optimize Taxes

- As a general rule of thumb, use the least flexible sources of income first while you're in the lowest tax brackets (e.g., OAS, CPP, work pensions).

- When income climbs into higher tax brackets, be strategic about which income sources to utilize (e.g., drawing funds from RRSP, RRIF, and TFSA, or dividends and capital gains from non-registered accounts).

Step 6: Review & Adjust Annually

- Markets, interest rates, and tax law changes.

- Annual check-ins with an advisor to adjust to new realities.

The Cash Wedge: Creating Income Security in Uncertain Markets

One of the biggest concerns for retirees is ensuring guaranteed income, especially during market downturns. A GIC ladder, also known as the "cash wedge," provides a safety net by structuring 3 to 4 years of guaranteed income in safe or low-risk investments.

This strategy balances long-term growth with short-term security, ensuring retirees never have to sell at the worst possible time.

How a GIC Ladder Works:

1. **Assign your 1-year income needs** (the amount required from personal investments after other sources of income) into a HISA (High Interest Savings Account) or liquid interest cash account.

2. **Buy a 1-year GIC:** This GIC matures in one year and becomes your cash for lifestyle expenses.

3. **Buy a 2-year GIC:** In one year, this GIC will mature and become your 1-year GIC.

4. **Buy a 3-year GIC:** In one year, this GIC will mature and become your 2-year GIC.

5. Every fall, meet with your advisor to decide whether to buy another 3-year GIC to keep the ladder topped up or if market conditions are unfavourable, consider waiting a year or two for the portfolio to recover before rebuilding the wedge.

Remember, you have a 3 to 4-year buffer to wait for markets to recover.

Welcome to the Rollercoaster - Please Keep Your Hands Inside the Retirement Plan

Market volatility is a normal and expected part of investing, especially in retirement. Understanding what typically happens during different types of market downturns can help reduce stress and create confidence in your plan.

For example, markets regularly experience small dips of 0–5% several times a year, typically recovering within a few weeks.

Larger pullbacks of 5–10% usually happen once a year and rebound within a few months.

Corrections in the 10–19% range occur roughly every two to three years and recover in 6-12 months on average.

Full-blown bear markets (defined as drops of 20% or more) tend to happen on average every four years and can take one to three years to fully recover.

While these are historical averages and each market event is unique, they help frame expectations and highlight the importance of having a strategy in place. This is why a well-structured cash wedge—three to four years of secure, low-risk income—is so critical. It gives retirees the breathing room to ride out market volatility without having to sell long-term investments at a loss, ultimately allowing time, strategy, and discipline to work in their favour.

Two helpful examples highlight just how differently these market events can play out:

1. During the COVID-19 pandemic, of early 2020, markets dropped more than 30% in a matter of weeks—but recovered to pre-crash levels in under six months. Those who didn't have a cash wedge and pulled out of the markets missed one of the quickest bear market recoveries in history.

2. By contrast, the 2008 financial crisis saw some international markets fall over 50% and take more than two years to recover fully.

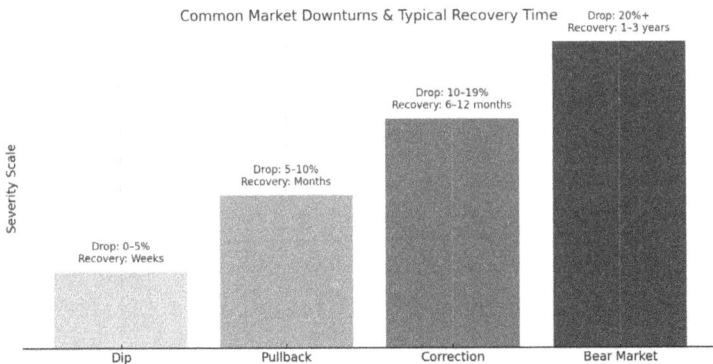

Common Market Downturns & Typical Recovery Time

Severity Scale

Drop: 0-5%
Recovery: Weeks

Drop: 5-10%
Recovery: Months

Drop: 10-19%
Recovery: 6-12 months

Drop: 20%+
Recovery: 1-3 years

Dip   Pullback   Correction   Bear Market

Disclaimer: This chart is for illustrative purposes only and does not represent actual market performance. It is intended to provide a general understanding of historical averages and should not be relied upon for investment decisions. Past performance is not indicative of future results. Always consult a qualified financial professional before making investment choices.

Why This Works

The Cash Wedge strategy prevents panic selling, eliminating the need to sell stocks during market crashes. Ensuring you always have cash available to cover 3 to 4 years of lifestyle expenses provides a safety net that allows you to weather financial uncertainty. It lets long-term investments, such as stocks and real estate, grow without being affected by short-term market volatility, giving them the time and space to ride out fluctuations and appreciate in value. This strategy balances the income certainty needs of this stage of life with the longevity needs of the rising cost of living.

The Situation: Blake and Alex retired in 2021 with a well-diversified portfolio. They understood that market downturns are inevitable, so they planned their cash flow strategy accordingly.

The Strategy: They implemented a cash wedge, keeping enough cash as well as 1, 2 and 3-year GICs to cover multiple years of living expenses that are required above and beyond what their CPP, OAS and work pensions cover. When markets dropped in 2022, they didn't panic-sell their investments. Instead, they relied on their cash wedge reserves to meet their needs while allowing their investments time to recover.

The Outcome: By 2024, the market had rebounded to all-time highs. Blake and Alex were able to replenish their year

2 and 3 cash wedge GICs by selling investments at a favourable time rather than being forced to sell at a loss during the downturn.

The Lesson: A well-structured cash wedge protects retirees from making emotional investment decisions during market volatility. By having a buffer, they can weather downturns without selling assets at depressed prices, ultimately preserving long-term wealth.

Final Thoughts on Turning Wealth into Reliable Income

While it's possible to structure your retirement income on your own, the reality is that it's often best done with the guidance of a professional financial advisor. Retirement income planning isn't a one-time event. It requires ongoing adjustments as tax laws change, market conditions shift, and personal circumstances evolve. What works one year may need fine-tuning the next to optimize taxation, manage risk, and ensure your income remains sustainable. A well-structured plan provides peace of mind, but regular reviews and proactive adjustments are what keep it working effectively over the long term. Whether you choose to do this yourself or work with an advisor, the key is to treat your retirement income strategy as a living plan that evolves alongside your retirement journey.

"It's not how much money you make,
but how much money you keep."
- Robert Kiyosaki.

Chapter 9:

The Hidden Cost of Selling in Retirement

In this chapter, we will discuss selling real estate in retirement, a significant financial decision that can impact your taxes, income, and overall retirement plan. Whether you're downsizing, cashing in on an investment property, or simplifying your estate, understanding the financial implications is essential. We will cover the following topics: Old Age Security (OAS) clawback, the "Gap Year Strategy," mortgage prepayment penalties, closing costs, appraisals, timing, and ways to optimize the sale.

Primary Residence vs. Secondary Property

When selling your primary residence, you won't be subject to capital gains tax due to the Principal Residence Exemption. However, selling a rental or secondary property means that 50% of the capital gain is taxable, which can significantly increase your taxable income.

OAS Clawback: The Cost of Capital Gains in Retirement

Many retirees don't realize that selling real estate can trigger a temporary loss of Old Age Security (OAS) benefits due to the OAS clawback (also known as the OAS Recovery Tax).

How the OAS Clawback Works

OAS benefits are reduced if your net income exceeds the annual threshold set by the CRA. In 2025, the clawback begins at an annual income of $93,454, and OAS benefits are fully eliminated when income reaches $157,490. It's important to note that when you sell a property, 50% of the capital gain is added to your income for the year, which could push you into the clawback range.

The Situation: Doug and Jesse, a retired couple in their early 70s, owned a rental property that had appreciated significantly in value. They decided to sell the property to simplify their lives and reinvest the proceeds into more liquid investments. Since they had already stopped working, they relied primarily on CPP, OAS, and withdrawals from their retirement accounts to cover their expenses. They weren't expecting any major financial disruptions.

The Strategy: Without considering the tax implications, Doug and Jesse listed and sold their rental property for a $400,000 gain. Because only 50% of the capital gain is taxable, $200,000 was added to their income for the year. Normally, their combined income was about $80,000—well below the OAS clawback threshold. However, because they were joint owners of the property, the capital gain was split evenly, adding $100,000 in taxable income to each of them, bringing their individual taxable incomes to approximately $140,000 each (including their $40,000 in usual pension and investment income).

Although this didn't push either of them over the full clawback threshold of $157,490 (2025), it placed both of them well above the initial OAS clawback threshold of $93,454, meaning a significant portion of their OAS payments for the following year would be clawed back.

The Outcome: As a result of the sale, Doug and Jesse:

1. Lost a substantial portion of their OAS benefits for the following year due to the income-based clawback. While it wasn't a complete clawback, it still represented a meaningful and unexpected reduction in their retirement income.

2. Were required to prepay taxes for the following year. Because their taxable income spiked, the CRA projected their income would stay high and requested quarterly tax installments—something they had never had to deal with before.

3. Faced a higher marginal tax rate, they paid significantly more on the capital gain than they would have in a lower-income year.

The Lesson: Even when jointly owned, selling a secondary property in retirement can trigger unintended financial consequences. Doug and Jesse didn't lose all of their OAS, but the clawback still hurt. When your retirement income is carefully balanced, even a partial clawback can feel like a pay cut. Add to that higher taxes and surprise CRA demands, and it becomes clear: timing matters.

To minimize the impact of the OAS clawback, you can spread out the gain over multiple years by structuring the sale as a vendor take-back mortgage or using a staggered sale approach. Managing withdrawals from RRSPs or TFSAs can also help, as adjusting your withdrawals in the years before and after the sale can smooth out taxable income. Additionally, charitable donations, RRSP contributions (if eligible), or carrying forward previous capital losses can reduce your overall taxable income and soften the impact of the sale.

The Gap Year Strategy™: Selling at the Right Time to Minimize Taxes

Over the years, I've met with many retirees who were surprised, and often disheartened, by how much tax they owed after selling a rental property. In some cases, they'd walk away with significantly less than they had expected simply because the sale happened at the wrong time. After seeing this situation play out again and again, I developed what I call the Gap Year Strategy.

This strategy is all about timing the sale of your rental or secondary property to minimize taxes and preserve more of your wealth. The ideal window is the year immediately after you retire but before you begin drawing income from your pension, CPP (Canada Pension Plan), or OAS. For example, if you retire in December, plan to sell your property in January—just one month later—and delay receiving any government benefits until the following year.

By creating a "Gap Year," where your income is lower than usual, you can reduce your overall tax burden and take advantage of several important financial benefits:

- OAS Clawback Protection: In 2025, the OAS clawback begins once your income exceeds $93,454. By selling in a low-income year, you can avoid triggering a reduction or complete loss of your OAS payments.

- Lower Capital Gains Tax: Since 50% of a capital gain is added to your income, selling while still receiving employment or pension income can push you into a higher tax bracket. In a gap year with minimal other income, the tax on that gain can be substantially lower.

- Boosted Government Benefits: Delaying CPP and OAS for even one year increases your benefits by roughly 6%, as both payments rise the longer you wait (up to age 70).

It's a proactive move that often flies under the radar, but when done properly, it can result in tens of thousands of dollars in savings and give you more control over your retirement cash flow.

Like any strategy, the Gap Year Strategy requires careful planning and coordination with your advisor or accountant. But the results can be well worth it: lower taxes, preserved government benefits, and a smoother financial transition into retirement.

One Step Further: Managing RRSP Room

To further enhance the Gap Year Strategy, proactively manage your RRSP contributions leading up to the sale of the property. By planning ahead, you and your spouse can contribute sale proceeds to your RRSP, potentially offsetting the taxable capital gains from selling your rental property. If large enough contribution room is available, your RRSP contribution could shelter much—or even all—of the capital gain, deferring tax on that income.

If you have disposable income before implementing the strategy, consider paying down debt or contributing to tax-advantaged accounts like a Tax-Free Savings Account (TFSA).

The Situation: John and Sarah own a rental property that has appreciated significantly over time. They are planning to retire but are concerned about the tax consequences of selling the property. If they sell in their final year of employment, the capital gain will be added to their salary, rental income, and investment earnings, pushing them into a high tax bracket and increasing their tax bill. Selling after starting CPP and OAS would cause their OAS to be clawed back due to their higher income.

The Strategy: Instead of selling before or immediately after retirement, John and Sarah retire in December and wait until January of the following year to sell their rental property. By doing this, their taxable income for that year consists mainly of the capital gain from the property sale rather than being stacked on top of their salary, pension income, and rental earnings. They also delay taking CPP and OAS to prevent adding those benefits to their income in the year of the sale, avoiding an unnecessary OAS clawback and actually increasing the CPP and OAS by close to 7% indefinitely!

The Outcome: By timing the sale, John and Sarah keep their taxable income lower, which reduces the capital gains tax compared to selling while still employed. Additionally, by delaying CPP and OAS, they avoid the OAS clawback, preserving their retirement benefits. This approach saves them thousands in taxes and helps them maximize their retirement income.

The Lesson: Selling a rental property in retirement requires careful planning to minimize taxes and avoid OAS clawbacks. By timing the sale in a lower-income year before receiving government benefits, retirees can reduce their tax burden, keep more of their sale proceeds, and protect their retirement income. This strategy ensures a smoother financial transition and preserves both real estate wealth and government benefits.

Let's compare the impact of selling a rental property in two different income years using British Columbia's 2025 personal tax rates.

Scenario 1: Selling in a High-Income Year (Income: $120,000)

- Total income: $120,000 (earned income)
- Capital gain: $200,000
- Total taxable income: $320,000
- Estimated total tax paid: $122,142.61

Scenario 2: Selling in a Low-Income Year (Income: $0)

- Total income: $0 (earned income)

- Capital gain: $200,000

- Total taxable income: $200,000

- Estimated total tax paid: $46,184.72

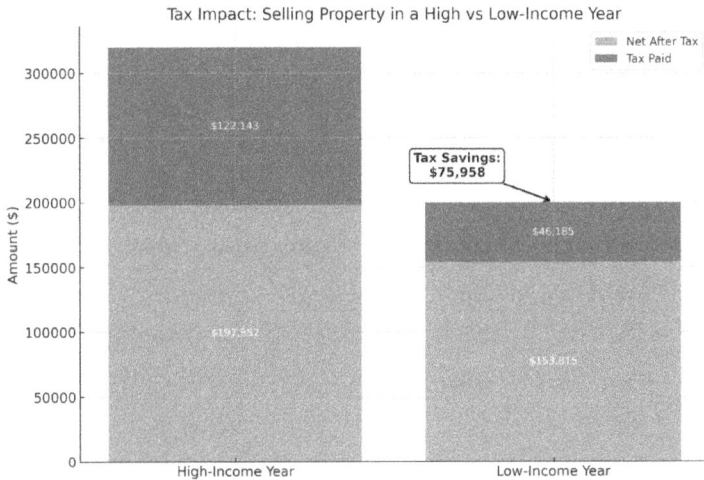

Tax Impact: Selling Property in a High vs Low-Income Year

Comparison: By selling the property in a year with no earned income, John and Sarah save $75,957.89 in taxes, compared to selling in a high-income year. This illustrates the significant tax advantage of timing the sale in a low-income year.

Important Notes: The tax amounts presented are simplified estimates based on the 2025 BC tax brackets and should be verified with a tax professional for precise calculations. The savings and outcomes will vary based on specific circumstances, including other deductions, credits, and planning strategies.

Mortgage Penalties: The Price of Selling Too Soon

When selling a home with an outstanding mortgage, you may face prepayment penalties, especially if you have a fixed-rate mortgage. These penalties can be significant and should be considered in your decision.

Fixed vs. Variable Rate Mortgage Penalties

- **Variable Rate Mortgage:** The penalty is typically 3 months' interest.

- **Fixed Rate Mortgage:** The penalty is either 3 months' interest or the Interest Rate Differential (IRD), whichever is higher. The IRD is the difference between your current mortgage rate and the rate at which the lender could lend the remaining term of your mortgage.

To avoid these costs, one option is to port your mortgage when purchasing a new home. Many lenders allow you to transfer your existing mortgage to the new property without breaking the original terms, allowing you to maintain your interest rate and avoid penalties. Alternatively, waiting until your mortgage term expires to make any changes can give you the opportunity to switch lenders or renegotiate terms without incurring a penalty.

It's also worth checking your mortgage for prepayment options. Some lenders allow lump-sum payments of 10-20% of the principal each year without penalty. By making these extra payments, you can gradually reduce your balance and avoid a hefty fee if you decide to break your mortgage early.

The Situation: You have a fixed-rate mortgage with a remaining balance of $400,000 and an interest rate of 4%. With current mortgage rates at 2%, breaking your mortgage early triggers a penalty based on the Interest Rate Differential (IRD), which could amount to $15,000 to $20,000. If you had a variable-rate mortgage instead, the penalty would typically be much lower, around $3,000 to $4,000.

The Strategy: Before making a prepayment or breaking a mortgage early, it's important to understand how penalties are calculated. Fixed-rate mortgages often use the Interest Rate Differential, which compares your contracted rate with current market rates, potentially leading to a significant penalty. In contrast, variable-rate mortgages usually have a three-month interest penalty, which tends to be more manageable. One way to reduce penalties is to make lump-sum prepayments within the lender's allowed limits before breaking the mortgage. Another approach is to blend and extend the mortgage, rolling the remaining balance into a new term at a lower rate without incurring a full penalty.

The Outcome: Without planning, breaking a fixed-rate mortgage early could result in a penalty of tens of thousands of dollars, significantly reducing any savings from refinancing. However, by understanding the penalty structure, exploring prepayment options, or negotiating a blend-and-extend, borrowers can minimize costs and take advantage of lower interest rates more efficiently.

The Lesson: Mortgage prepayment penalties can be costly, especially for fixed-rate borrowers, when interest rates drop. Before making any decisions, it's crucial to understand your mortgage terms, calculate potential penalties, and explore alternative strategies to avoid unnecessary expenses. Proper planning can help you maximize savings while keeping more of your money working for you.

Closing Cost: The Hidden Fees to Watch For

When selling a home it's crucial to account for the hidden costs associated with closing the transaction. One of the largest expenses is realtor commissions, which in British Columbia typically amount to 6% on the first $100,000 of the sale price and 3% on the balance, usually split between the buyer's and seller's agents. While commissions can sometimes be negotiated, this remains a significant cost when selling your home.

In addition to realtor fees, legal fees for the sale typically range from $1,000 to $3,000. These fees cover the preparation of documents and ensure that the legal transfer of ownership is carried out properly. If you have a mortgage remaining on the property, prepayment penalties may apply. These penalties can vary, but typically, they are either 3 months of interest or the Interest Rate Differential (IRD), whichever is higher, depending on the terms of your mortgage.

For those selling secondary properties, capital gains tax is another potential expense. The tax is calculated on the profit made from the sale of the property and can vary based on your individual tax situation, so it's essential to consult with a tax professional. In addition to these costs, moving expenses can range from $1,000 to $5,000, depending on the distance and size of your move. This includes hiring professional movers or renting a truck and transporting your belongings to your new home.

Finally, home repairs and staging may be necessary to make the property more appealing to buyers, especially in a competitive market. Depending on the extent of repairs or improvements, this can cost anywhere from $5,000 to $15,000. Staging, although optional, can also be a valuable investment to help present the home in its best light and potentially increase its sale price. Understanding these various closing costs and planning for them in advance is essential to avoid surprises and ensure a successful and profitable sale.

Breakdown of Common Closing Costs

Cost	Typical Range	Example (Home Sold for $800,000)
Realtor Commissions	6% on the first 100k and 3% on the balance. (split between buyer & seller agents)	$27,000.00
Legal Fees	$1,000 - $3,000	$2,000
Mortgage Penalty	Varies (see previous section)	$10,000
Capital Gains Tax (if applicable)	Varies based on property and gains	$30,000+
Moving Costs	$1,000 - $5,000	$3,000
Home Repairs / Staging	Optional but recommended	$5,000 - $15,000
Total Potential Costs	$50,000 - $100,000+	$52,000+

Selling Privately vs. Using a Realtor: Pros and Cons

When deciding whether to sell your home privately or with a realtor, it's important to weigh the pros and cons of each approach.

Selling privately allows you to avoid paying the typical realtor commission fees, which can be a significant saving, but it also means you take on the responsibility of marketing the home, handling negotiations, and managing legal requirements on your own. Selling privately can save you thousands in commissions, but it requires expertise in pricing, negotiations, and contracts. Without proper marketing, sellers risk pricing too low and leaving money on the table.

A realtor brings market insights, handles negotiations, and manages legal complexities—often leading to a smoother and more profitable sale. Realtors also have access to a larger network of buyers and can help ensure that the sale goes smoothly with fewer potential legal risks. However, the cost of their services, typically around 6% on the first $100,000 and 3% on the remainder of the sale price, must be factored into your decision.

The Situation: Maria and Juan are considering selling their home. They've heard about the potential savings of selling privately and are wondering if this is a feasible option for them. Their home is located in a popular neighbourhood, and they believe there may be high demand.

The Strategy: They decide to list the home privately, avoiding realtor fees. They use online listings and social media to market the property and handle inquiries directly.

The Outcome: While they do manage to attract interest and find a buyer, the process is more time-consuming than they anticipated. They spend hours showing the house, negotiating the sale, and dealing with paperwork. Although they saved on realtor commissions, they ended up spending a significant amount of time and effort and faced some challenges with the legal complexities of the transaction. Additionally, they sold the house for less than comparable homes sold through realtors in the area due to a lack of professional marketing.

The Lesson: Selling privately can work for some, especially if you're familiar with the process and market conditions. However, it's crucial to consider the time, effort, and expertise required to handle all aspects of the sale. Using a realtor may cost more in commissions, but it often results in a smoother, quicker sale and could potentially net a higher price due to professional marketing and negotiation skills.

Stage 3:

Stage 3:

Estate Planning
- Keeping Real Estate
in the Family
(The Right Way)

Last year, I sat across from three adult siblings who had just lost their father. He'd worked hard his entire life, built a successful career, and invested wisely. He'd purchased a lakefront vacation home where the family had spent summers for decades. The property was filled with memories of barbecues on the deck, kids learning to swim off the dock, and late nights by the fire. It was, in their words, the heart of the family.

But as we started discussing the next steps, it became painfully clear that their father had never put a clear plan in place for the property. Two of the siblings wanted to keep it in the family, while the third—who lived in another province and had no interest in maintaining it—wanted to sell it. Emotions ran high, and what had been a source of joy quickly became a source of stress, tension, and resentment.

This isn't an uncommon story. Estate planning requires dividing assets while protecting relationships. Without a clear plan, a family cottage, rental property, or primary home can go from being a cherished legacy to a point of conflict. And yet, most people avoid these conversations until it's too late.

In this section, we'll explore how to pass down real estate the right way—whether that means gifting it during your lifetime, setting up joint ownership, using trusts, or selling with tax efficiency in mind. We'll also discuss common mistakes, proactive solutions, and how to have these important conversations before emotions take over. Because a well-planned legacy ensures your family remains wealthy in finances, love, and connection long after you're gone.

"When I pass, I want the government to decide what happens to my estate, and I trust them to make the best decisions regarding all my most treasured possessions."

- No one ever.

Chapter 10:

The Estate Plan You Didn't Choose (But Will Get Anyway)

What Happens if You Don't Plan?

An estate is everything a person owns at the time they pass away—money, property, belongings, and debts. It's what gets passed on to others through a will or estate plan. Without a basic estate plan in place, the quote at the beginning of this chapter is essentially what happens. The government has a predetermined set of rules dictating how your assets will be distributed, who will handle your affairs, and who will make decisions on your behalf if you become incapacitated or pass away. These default rules don't take your personal values, relationships, or unique intentions into account.

The good news? Setting up the basics of an estate plan is simpler and more affordable than many people assume. At the very least, you should have three key documents in place:

1. **A Will**: This legal document ensures your assets are distributed according to your wishes. Without a will, the government decides who gets what. This can lead to delays, legal battles, and unintended consequences.

2. **A Power of Attorney (POA)**: This appoints someone to manage your financial affairs if you become incapacitated. Without it, your loved ones may have to go through a lengthy and costly court process to gain authority over your finances.

3. **A Representation Agreement**: This document designates who will make healthcare decisions on your behalf if you're unable to do so. It's not always the same person

as your POA—you may want different individuals handling your finances and healthcare.

That's it! Three essential documents that provide clarity, control, and peace of mind for you and your loved ones. Putting them in place now can prevent unnecessary stress, legal fees, and confusion later.

Deemed Disposition Rule: Understanding The Tax Rules

In Canada, when a person passes away, their capital property (e.g., real estate, stocks, and private businesses) is deemed to be disposed of (sold) at Fair Market Value (FMV). As a result, any capital gains tax due on the increase in value since the property was acquired is payable on the final tax return.

Who Pays the Tax?

The estate is responsible for paying any capital gains tax before distributing assets to the beneficiaries. If the estate doesn't have enough liquid assets to cover the tax, the heirs may need to sell the property or use other estate assets to make the payment.

Assets Subject to Deemed Disposition

Several assets are subject to deemed disposition at the time of death, including real estate (except for the principal residence, which may qualify for tax exemption). Other taxable assets include investment portfolios such as stocks, bonds, ETFs, and mutual funds. Private corporations, business interests, rental properties, cottages, and even cryptocurrencies or alternative investments are subject to capital gains tax upon death.

Assets That Can Avoid Immediate Taxation

Certain assets may be exempt from immediate taxation or qualify for tax deferrals. The principal residence can be exempt from capital gains tax under the Principal Residence Exemption (PRE). Similarly, RRSPs and RRIFs can be rolled over tax-free to a surviving spouse, but if they are passed to children or non-spouse beneficiaries, they will be fully taxed. Some private businesses or farms may qualify for tax exemptions or deferrals. Life insurance policies are another exception. Death benefits from these policies are not taxable and can help offset estate taxes.

Principal Residence - No Tax Owed

If the house was the parent's principal residence, there would be no capital gains tax owed upon inheritance. The children would receive the property at its FMV at the time of the parent's death. If they later decide to sell the home and its value has increased, they may owe capital gains tax on the appreciation. However, they can avoid this tax if they choose to designate the property as their own principal residence.

Secondary Property (Cottage, Rental, Investment) - Taxable Event

If the property is a second home, rental, or investment property, capital gains tax will apply. When a person passes away, the CRA treats their assets as if they were sold at FMV just before death. This means the estate may owe capital gains tax on the increase in the property's value since the time it was originally purchased.

The Situation: Cho and Mei bought a cottage for $200,000. At the time of their death, its FMV increased to $600,000.

The Strategy: The cottage's capital gain of $400,000 was realized and the estate owes taxes on 50% of this gain. $200,000 will be taxed at the estate's marginal tax rate.

The Outcome: The estate was faced with a substantial tax liability, reducing the amount left for the beneficiaries after taxes.

The Lesson: Without proper estate planning or consideration of tax implications, significant capital gains taxes can be triggered. This reduces the value of the estate passed down to heirs. It's essential to plan for these taxes in advance, especially with appreciating assets like real estate.

Strategies for Deferring Taxes on Property Transfers

The principal residence exemption can be applied if the parents own multiple properties. The estate can choose which property to apply the exemption to. If a surviving spouse inherits the property there is no immediate tax, as it is deferred until they sell or pass away. Options like joint ownership, trusts, or gifting strategies may help reduce taxes, though these require careful planning to avoid unintended consequences.

Tax Deferral Strategies for Wealthy Families

Since Canada does not offer a Step-Up in value at death, wealthy families often use legal strategies to delay or reduce taxes. This helps them pass on more of their wealth without paying large amounts right away.

Spousal Rollover (Tax Deferral for Spouses)

Capital property can be transferred tax-free to a spouse at the Adjusted Cost Base (ACB), which avoids an immediate tax bill. An ACB is what someone paid for an investment or property, plus legal fees and commissions. This may change over time due to reinvested dividends or return of capital. The tax is deferred until the surviving spouse either sells the asset or passes away. This strategy is commonly used for investment portfolios, real estate, and private corporations.

The Situation: Coleen owns a rental property with a $500,000 ACB, and its current value is $1.5 million. If Coleen passes away, there would typically be a $1 million capital gain, resulting in $500,000 of taxable income.

The Strategy: However, by leaving the property to her spouse, Coleen can defer the tax liability. No tax is due at the time of her death until her spouse either sells the property or passes away.

The Outcome: Coleen's spouse inherits the property without an immediate tax burden, allowing the deferred tax to be addressed later, potentially under more favourable circumstances.

The Lesson: Proper estate planning can help minimize or defer tax liabilities, such as capital gains taxes, by using strategies like leaving property to a spouse. This ensures the heirs or spouse in this case aren't burdened with taxes immediately, giving them more flexibility in managing the property.

Estate Freezes: Keeping Wealth in The Family

An estate freeze is a way to lock in the current value of something you own so that any future growth can go to your family without causing a big tax bill right away. This method is often used with shares in a private business, but it can also work for real estate. It's helpful for people who want to pass on the future appreciation of a property to their heirs while still keeping control over it.

The Situation: Jane and Tom, a married couple in their early 60s, have owned a commercial property worth $2 million in downtown Victoria, which they've held for over 20 years. They're thinking about giving the property to their children but want to keep control and avoid a big tax bill. They're also worried the property will keep going up in values, so they want to lock in today's price for tax purposes.

The Strategy: Jane and Tom decide to implement an estate freeze by transferring the property into a family trust. In this scenario, they freeze the value of the property at $2 million, which is the current market value. Any increase in the property's value above 2 million will go to their children. Jane and Tom still keep control of the property, but the trust makes sure the future growth goes to the next generation. This way, they avoid paying tax on the property's future increase in value.

The Outcome: By freezing the current value of the property, Jane and Tom can pass on the future increase in the property's value to their children without having to pay taxes on it right away. The trust allows them to maintain control over the property's operations while their children benefit from the property's future growth. This strategy reduces the amount of capital gains taxes that their heirs would need to pay upon receiving the property, as only the initial $2 million value is considered in the tax calculation.

The Lesson: An estate freeze in real estate can be an effective strategy for locking in the current value of a property for tax purposes while transferring any future growth to heirs. By utilizing a family trust structure, individuals can keep control of their real estate assets and future estate taxes. It's important to set things up properly to make sure the strategy works and follows tax rules.

Life Insurance as a Tool For Covering Tax Liabilities

Wealthy individuals often purchase permanent life insurance policies to provide a tax-free payout that can cover capital gains taxes due upon death. The payout goes directly to the estate or the heirs, ensuring that no assets need to be liquidated to cover the tax liability.

The Situation: David owns a $3 million investment property, and his estimated tax liability upon death is $750,000. He wants to ensure his family doesn't have to sell the property to cover these taxes.

The Strategy: David buys a life insurance policy that pays $750,000 tax-free to his estate, providing funds to cover the tax liability without needing to sell the property.

The Outcome: When David passes away, the life insurance policy pays the $750,000 tax-free to his estate, allowing his family to keep the investment property intact without the need for a forced sale to pay taxes.

The Lesson: Using life insurance to cover tax liabilities upon death is a way to preserve family wealth, especially when it comes to valuable assets like real estate or family businesses. It's important to plan ahead so your children can inherit them without facing a big financial burden.

Corporate-Owned Life Insurance:
COLI (For Real Estate Business Owners)

Corporate-Owned Life Insurance "COLI" is when a business buys a life insurance policy on one of its key people, usually an owner or shareholder. The company pays the premiums and receives the payout when that person passess away. This can help the business grow money in a tax friendly way, cover future expenses, and provide cash when it's needed most. For real estate investors, COLI can be a smart way to plan their estate, protect their assets, and pass on wealth to their family all while keeping the business or property running smoothly.

The Situation: James, a successful real estate investor in his 60s, owns a portfolio of rental properties valued at $15 million, which he plans to pass on to his children. He wants to make sure the properties are well-maintained and managed after his death, but he also wants to provide his heirs with liquidity to cover taxes or any debts without having to sell the properties. James is seeking a strategy that allows him to preserve the wealth within the family while minimizing the financial burden on his children.

The Strategy: James sets up a COLI policy, with his real estate corporation as the policyholder. The corporation purchases a life insurance policy for James' life and continues to pay the premiums. The death benefit from the policy is structured to provide the corporation with the necessary liquidity to pay for any estate taxes, debts, or other liabilities associated with James' passing. This ensures that his children can inherit the properties without being forced to sell them to cover expenses. The policy grows tax-deferred, creating a tax-efficient asset within the corporation.

The Outcome: When James passes away, the corporation receives the death benefit from the life insurance policy, providing the necessary cash to cover any estate-related expenses, including taxes, without having to liquidate his real estate holdings. His children inherit the real estate portfolio intact, and the estate can be settled smoothly. The tax-deferred growth of the life insurance policy allows the corporation to maintain its operations, including management and property maintenance, without disruption.

The Lesson: For real estate investors, a Corporate-Owned Life Insurance policy can be an effective way to pass property holdings to children or heirs in a way that keeps taxes low and makes cash available when needed. By incorporating COLI into their estate planning strategy, property owners can avoid forced sales of assets, reduce financial stress for heirs, and create a tax-efficient legacy.

Family Trusts: When They Make Sense

A family trust is a legal arrangement where a person (the settlor) puts assets under the control of a trustee to manage them for the benefit of specific family members (the beneficiaries). This can be a forward thinking way to manage real estate assets by deferring taxes and enabling income splitting. With the right structure, a family trust can provide tax-efficient distribution of real estate income and capital gains to heirs over time. A trust has the added benefit of avoiding probate.

A family trust can be used on its own, without an estate freeze as we discussed earlier, to hold and manage assets for the benefit of family members. This offers flexibility, protection, and estate planning advantages.

An estate freeze is a separate strategy that is often combined with a family trust when you want to lock in today's value of a growing business or asset and shift future growth to the next generation.

Let's look at when a family trust without an estate freeze makes sense.

The Situation: Fatima and Omar own $5 million worth of rental properties and want to pass them on to their children. They're looking for a way to do it that keeps taxes as low as possible.

The Strategy: They work with a lawyer to place the rental property portfolio into a family trust. The trust distributes rental income and capital gains among family members in a tax friendly way, benefiting those in lower tax brackets.

The Outcome: The family trust allows the investor to defer capital gains taxes over an extended period, reducing immediate tax liabilities. The trust also provides the heirs with income splitting benefits, lowering the overall tax burden during the transfer of wealth. Over time, the family can enjoy ongoing benefits from the properties with a reduced tax impact.

The Lesson: Placing real estate assets into a family trust is great for deferring taxes, managing capital gains, and facilitating income splitting of rental revenue. This approach helps preserve wealth, minimizes tax, and ensures that future generations benefit from the assets long term.

Borrowing Against Assets: A Little-Known Strategy

For wealthy individuals, borrowing against assets can provide liquidity without triggering immediate taxes, particularly capital gains taxes. By leveraging the value of their assets, such as real estate or investments, individuals can access funds for personal needs, business investments, or estate planning purposes without reducing the value of their estate through asset sales. This strategy helps maintain wealth within the estate and can also reduce the taxable estate by ensuring that any loans are repaid using tax-advantaged assets, like life insurance, upon the individual's passing.

This approach keeps properties intact while delaying taxes, providing a significant advantage for future generations. Proper succession planning seamlessly passes wealth without triggering unnecessary taxes or forcing heirs to liquidate valuable assets.

The Situation: William, a seasoned real estate investor in his early 70s, owns a collection of properties valued at $10 million. He wants to avoid selling any of his properties, as he is emotionally attached to them and doesn't want to incur capital gains tax on their appreciation. However, William needs liquidity to cover his lifestyle expenses in retirement and to invest in a life insurance policy that would help support his estate planning. He's looking for a way to access funds without triggering a taxable event.

The Strategy: Instead of selling one of his properties, William decides to take out a loan against the equity in his real estate holdings. He borrows $2 million from a financial institution, using his properties as collateral. He uses this loan to cover his lifestyle expenses and to purchase a life insurance policy, with the intention of using the policy's death benefit to repay the loan after his passing. By borrowing the funds rather than selling the properties, William avoids paying capital gains tax on the appreciated value of the real estate. Upon his death, the estate will repay the loan with the proceeds from the life insurance, reducing the overall taxable value of his estate.

The Outcome: When William passes away, the life insurance policy's death benefit is used to pay off the $2 million loan. His real estate holdings remain intact and his heirs inherit the properties without the need to sell them. Furthermore, the estate's taxable value is reduced, as the loan repayment is covered by the tax-advantaged life insurance benefit, thus deferring the tax owed. This allows his heirs to inherit the assets with minimal tax impact and no forced sales.

The Lesson: By borrowing against assets instead of liquidating them, William effectively avoids immediate capital gains tax while keeping his portfolio intact. He invests in life insurance to guarantee that the loan is repaid in a tax-efficient manner, reducing the taxable estate. For real estate owners and other wealthy individuals, using debt as a tool for estate planning allows them to access necessary liquidity without diminishing the value of their estate or triggering immediate taxes.

"If you want to know the true nature of a man, share an inheritance with him."

- Mark Twain.

Chapter 11:

How to Pass Down Property Without Creating a Family Feud

Transferring real estate to the next generation is often more complex than families anticipate. Many people assume their wishes will be carried out smoothly, but without proper planning, disputes, unexpected taxes, and legal complications can arise. This chapter explores the right ways to pass down property while avoiding common mistakes.

The Most Common Estate Planning Mistakes (and How to Avoid Them)

Family disputes over inherited property are often the result of poor communication, unclear expectations, or a lack of formal planning. One of the most frequent mistakes parents make is assuming that dividing assets equally among their children will be fair. While this may seem like the logical approach, it doesn't always work when it comes to real estate. Unlike cash, property can't be easily split between siblings, and this can lead to significant conflicts. For instance, if one child wants to keep the property and the others want to sell it, it can cause resentment and emotional strain. Therefore, it's crucial to consider the unique needs and desires of each child before making decisions about inheritance.

Another common mistake is not clarifying who will be responsible for ongoing property expenses such as taxes, insurance, and maintenance. When a home is inherited by multiple heirs, it's important to set clear expectations about who will cover these costs. Without a formal agreement, confusion and financial strain can quickly lead to disagreements. Similarly, many parents assume their children will "figure it out" on their own when it comes to inheritance matters. However, without clear instructions, misunderstandings can arise, often resulting in costly court battles and tax inefficiencies that could have been avoided with proper planning.

I often discuss clients' intentions for their real estate, particularly when it comes to passing property down to their children. A common response is that they want to leave it to them. However, clients often mention that one child lives in a different town, starting a family, while another already owns a home nearby. I ask, "Given this, have you considered if they actually want your property? How will they share costs, handle maintenance, or manage renting it out?" These questions help clients realize that, while they assume their children would want the property, the reality is that their children may not be interested in taking on the responsibility and might choose to sell it instead.

It's important to have open and honest conversations with heirs about intentions and expectations before any decisions are made. Creating a detailed estate plan with clear instructions for the distribution and management of assets ensures that all parties are on the same page. If necessary, seeking the help of a mediator can help facilitate these discussions, ensuring fairness and preventing conflicts among family members. By addressing these issues ahead of time, parents can help ensure that their legacy is passed on smoothly and without unnecessary disputes.

A key strategy in estate planning for clients is to maximize the property for their own enjoyment and lifestyle at this stage of life. This shift in thinking allows them to make the most of their real estate for their current desires, whether that means keeping it or selling it to better align with their own needs. Many find that selling the property or repurposing it for their own use brings them more enjoyment and financial flexibility instead of worrying about what the children might want down the road or, rather, might not want. It's important to have open conversations about these topics to ensure decisions are made based on current realities, not assumptions. This can lead to more fulfilling decisions for both the parents and their children.

What is Probate?

Probate is the legal process of validating a will and distributing an estate. In Canada, probate fees (also called estate administration taxes) vary by province but can be as high as 1.5% of the estate's value. While Canada does not have a formal estate tax, capital gains tax on real estate can be a significant cost upon death, particularly if multiple properties are involved.

Gifting vs. Selling vs. Inheritance: Which is Best?

How you transfer real estate impacts taxation, legal rights, and family dynamics. Here's how each method works:

Gifting Real Estate

When gifting real estate, there are both advantages and disadvantages. On the positive side, gifting real estate can avoid probate and ensure the transfer occurs during the owner's lifetime. However, it also triggers immediate capital gains tax unless the property is a principal residence. Legally, it's important to document the gift properly to prevent potential disputes among heirs or beneficiaries.

The Situation: Lisa owns a rental condo that she originally purchased for $300K, and its current value is $700K. After considering her options, Lisa decides to gift the condo to her daughter.

The Strategy: Lisa gifts the condo to her daughter, which means she avoids the property going through probate and ensures the transfer occurs during her lifetime. However, since it's not her principal residence, the gift triggers a capital gains tax.

The Outcome: Lisa reports a $400K capital gain ($700K current value minus $300K original purchase price) and pays tax on 50% of the gain. Her daughter now owns the condo, but she now owes taxes on 50% of the capital gains as the property is deemed dispossessed even though she didn't sell it.

The Lesson: While gifting real estate can be a way to ensure assets are passed on during one's lifetime and avoid probate, it's important to understand that doing so may trigger immediate capital gains tax, which could be significant if the property has appreciated in value.

Selling Property to Family

Selling secondary property to a family member has its pros and cons. On the positive side, it can create fairness among heirs and allow for structured payments. However, selling to a family member also triggers capital gains tax, and the buyer may owe land transfer tax. The sale should occur at fair market value to avoid scrutiny from the Canada Revenue Agency (CRA).

The Situation: Mark decides to sell his rental to his son for $500K, even though its current market value is $800K. He believes this will help his son afford the property, but he is unaware of the potential tax consequences.

The Strategy: Mark sells the property below market value, but the CRA may consider this a below-market sale. As a result, Mark will be taxed as though he sold the property for $800K, even though he only received $500K. A better approach would be to use a vendor take-back mortgage, where Mark finances part of the sale at a fair price.

The Outcome: In this case, Mark is liable for taxes on the $300K capital gain (the difference between $800K and $500K). However, with a vendor take-back mortgage, Mark could structure the sale to ensure it is at fair market value, reducing potential tax liabilities.

The Lesson: It's important to consider the tax implications when selling property to a family member. Selling below market value can trigger unexpected tax consequences. Using tools like vendor take-back mortgages can help create a fair transaction while minimizing tax liabilities.

Leaving Property as an Inheritance

Leaving property as an inheritance can offer some benefits, such as deferring taxes until death, which allows the owner to maintain control of the property during their lifetime. However, the downside is that capital gains tax will be due upon death, which can place a financial burden on the estate. For legal reasons, it's important to specify the property distribution in the will, possibly with the help of a trust, to ensure clarity and prevent disputes.

The Situation: Sandra decides to leave her vacation home, valued at $1M, to her son in her will. She believes this will provide him with a valuable asset. However, Sandra is aware that upon her death, her estate will be responsible for paying capital gains tax on the increase in value since the time of purchase.

The Strategy: Upon Sandra's passing, her estate must pay the capital gains tax on the increase in value of the property. If there are insufficient liquid assets to cover the tax bill, the home may need to be sold to meet this obligation. To avoid this, Sandra purchased a life insurance policy to cover the estate taxes upon her death.

The Outcome: Sandra's estate will face a capital gains tax bill, but thanks to the life insurance policy, the tax burden will be covered without needing to sell the vacation home. The son can inherit the property without the added stress of selling it to pay the tax.

The Lesson: When leaving a secondary property as an inheritance, planning ahead can alleviate financial burdens and preserve family assets. Life insurance can be a strategic tool to cover estate taxes, ensuring that heirs receive the property without the need to sell it to settle taxes.

Method	Key Benefits	Tax Implications	Real-Life Example
Gifting During Lifetime	Avoids probate, immediate transfer.	Capital gains tax is due immediately on the gain; possible property transfer tax.	Parents gift a cottage to children, triggering a capital gains tax bill, but avoiding probate later.
Selling to Family	Allows structured payments, clear ownership.	Capital gains tax is due immediately on the sale; possible property transfer tax.	A father sells his home to his son at fair market value, using a vendor take-back mortgage to ease payments.
Inheritance Upon Death	Defers tax until the owner's passing, keeps control.	Deemed disposition rule applies; capital gains tax due on final return.	A rental property passes to heirs, and capital gains tax is paid by the estate before distribution.

Using Joint Ownership with Right of Survivorship

Joint ownership with the right of survivorship allows a property to automatically transfer to the surviving co-owner upon death, bypassing the probate process. While this can simplify the transfer, it may lead to tax consequences if not structured properly.

The Situation: A mother decides to add her son as a joint tenant to the title of her home. This is done with the intent that, upon her passing, the home will pass directly to her son without the need for probate.

The Strategy: The mother adds her son as a joint tenant, giving him the right of survivorship. This means that when she passes away, the property automatically transfers to him, avoiding probate. However, the CRA may view this as a partial gift, especially if the property has appreciated in value since it was purchased.

The Outcome: When the mother passes away, the home transfers to her son without the probate process, as planned. However, the CRA treats the transfer as a partial gift and applies capital gains tax on the appreciated value of the property after her death. This could result in taxes being owed for the son that he must address when he goes to sell in the future.

The Lesson: Joint ownership with rights of survivorship can simplify the transfer of property and avoid probate.

However, this strategy can also trigger capital gains tax on appreciated value.

Multigenerational Living:
The New Retirement Trend

As housing costs rise and families look for ways to support aging parents, more people are considering multigenerational living arrangements. In theory, this can be a win-win: elderly parents get to stay in a family environment while receiving care, and adult children benefit from pooled resources. However, without careful planning, these arrangements can lead to financial strain, tax implications, and even legal disputes. The key concerns revolve around ownership structure, estate planning, and long-term financial security.

Who will legally own the home? How will the parents' financial contributions be protected? What happens if family dynamics shift—if a parent requires long-term care or if a sibling has a future claim to the property? These questions should be addressed early on to prevent unintended consequences. The following example illustrates a situation where financial and legal challenges arose due to unclear planning.

The Situation: Elderly parents, Jim and Linda, spent decades in a home they owned outright in Saskatchewan. As they aged, they found it increasingly difficult to maintain the property and wanted to be closer to their adult son, Mark, who lived in British Columbia with his wife, Sarah. The couple decided to sell their home and contribute the proceeds toward a new house with Mark and Sarah, where they could live together and receive support in their later years. The plan also had an additional layer of complexity—Jim and Linda's other child, Jake, had lifelong challenges that limited his independence, and they hoped he would eventually live in the home after they passed.

To simplify financing, Mark and Sarah took out the mortgage in their names, while Jim and Linda contributed $500,000 from the sale of their home toward the purchase. The family assumed this arrangement would be straightforward, but over time, financial and legal complications emerged.

The Strategy: This family did not have a solid financial strategy. The assumption was that the family arrangement would work based on trust, but they did not formalize the parents' financial contribution in legal terms. Because Mark and Sarah were the only ones listed on the title, the house was legally considered theirs—even though Jim and Linda had invested a significant portion of their savings. From a tax perspective, Jim and Linda lost their principal residence exemption once they sold their home, meaning they no longer had a tax-free growth asset in their name. Meanwhile, if Mark and Sarah ever sold the home, capital gains taxes could apply to their parents' share of the investment.

The situation became even more complicated when Jim passed away unexpectedly. Linda, now the sole surviving parent, needed long-term care, and the family had to consider whether to sell the home to cover her medical costs.

However, because she was not on the title, she had no direct claim to the home's value. Additionally, Jake, who was supposed to inherit his parents' portion of the home, had no legal protection to ensure he could continue to live there. Mark and Sarah faced a difficult dilemma: should they legally formalize Jake's future ownership at the risk of complicating their mortgage obligations, or should they retain full ownership and risk family disputes down the road?

The Outcome: The family found themselves in a stressful legal battle when Linda's care costs became unmanageable. Mark and Sarah felt they had taken on the financial burden of homeownership and caregiving, while Jake argued that his parents' original investment should have secured him a place to live. Without clear legal agreements in place from the beginning, the family had to navigate a complex and emotional dispute, which ultimately resulted in Linda's share of the home being liquidated to cover her care. Jake was left without a guaranteed home, and tensions grew between the siblings over what was fair.

The Lesson: This situation highlights the importance of formalizing ownership, estate plans, and financial contributions before entering a multigenerational living arrangement. Families must clearly define whether parents' financial contributions are considered gifts, loans, or equity stakes in the property. They should also consider adding parents to the title, structuring the arrangement as co-ownership, or drafting a legal agreement that ensures fairness in case of future disputes. Long-term care planning must be factored in, as aging parents may need liquidity for medical expenses. When structuring a home purchase with multiple generations involved, estate planning should not be an afterthought—it should be integrated from day one to prevent misunderstandings and conflicts down the road.

Planning for Family-Owned Properties Without Drama

Careful planning is required when families jointly own properties, such as cottages or rental buildings, it's essential to implement careful planning to prevent disputes. The key areas to focus on include clear ownership agreements, succession planning, and tax planning.

The Situation: The Rodriguez family has owned a ski chalet for three generations. As the property passes down, there are potential risks of disagreements and confusion over the use and management of the property. To avoid future conflicts, the family decides to implement a co-ownership agreement.

The Strategy: The family creates a clear co-ownership agreement with the help of a lawyer that outlines each family member's rights to use the chalet, defines how the property can be sold (if someone wants to exit), and establishes a shared expense fund to cover maintenance costs. The agreement also specifies who will take over the management of the chalet in case the current owners pass away.

The Outcome: The chalet continues to be a cherished family asset, passed down through generations without legal conflicts or disagreements. The clear structure and agreement ensure that all family members understand their roles and responsibilities, and potential issues around property use or inheritance are avoided.

The Lesson: Clear estate planning, including ownership agreements and succession plans, is necessary for preserving family-owned properties. By outlining each member's rights, responsibilities, and the management of the property, families can avoid disputes and ensure the property remains a valued asset for future generations. Tax planning tools like trusts or life insurance can provide valuable solutions for funding estate taxes.

"A wise parent leaves their children enough to do something, but not enough to do nothing."
- Warren Buffett.

Chapter 12:

How to Talk to Your Family About Estate Planning

Discussing estate planning and property inheritance can be one of the most difficult conversations a family will have. Many parents avoid the topic because they don't want to create conflict or confront their own mortality. Children may hesitate to bring it up for fear of seeming greedy or insensitive. However, having these discussions early and openly is essential. Proactively addressing these matters can help prevent misunderstandings, legal battles, and financial burdens down the road.

To keep the conversation productive, parents need to remain open-minded. They should listen to their children's thoughts and concerns without feeling pressured. Equally, children must respect that the final decision rests with the parents. If disagreements arise during the discussion, the focus should be on understanding each other's perspectives rather than attempting to persuade the other party. It can also be helpful to hold one-on-one conversations with each child separately. This can reduce pressure and allow each child to feel like they have more of the parent's undivided attention.

If the conversation becomes difficult or emotionally charged, bringing in a neutral third party can be invaluable. A financial advisor, lawyer, or estate planner can help guide the discussion and prevent emotional arguments from taking over. In situations where family tensions are high, a mediator can provide structure and facilitate a more productive conversation.

It's critical to clearly document all decisions in a will or trust. Relying on verbal agreements can lead to confusion, disputes, and potential legal battles in the future. Having everything properly written down ensures that everyone is on the same page and that the wishes of the parents are honoured according to their intentions.

When to start the Conversation

The best time to start estate planning is now—before a crisis forces the conversation. Waiting until a health issue or other emergency arises can leave you or your loved ones unprepared, adding unnecessary stress and limiting your ability to make clear, informed decisions. Estate planning is most effective when done proactively, allowing you to structure your plan with a clear mind and ensure that your wishes are carried out exactly as intended. Taking action now means you stay in control, prevent rushed decisions, and provide your family with guidance and security for the future.

The Situation: Mark, a 68-year-old retiree, had been meaning to set up his estate plan but kept putting it off, thinking he had plenty of time. He wanted to update his will, assign a power of attorney, and discuss his wishes with his children, but life kept getting in the way. Then, unexpectedly, Mark suffered a severe stroke that left him unable to communicate. Without clear instructions in place, his family was left to make difficult financial and medical decisions without knowing what he truly wanted. His assets became tied up in legal complications, and tensions arose among his children regarding how to handle his care and estate.

The Strategy: Mark did not implement a solid financial strategy. Had he taken the time to complete his estate plan while he was in good health, he could have clearly documented his wishes, assigned a power of attorney to manage his finances and healthcare, and ensured a smooth transfer of assets. By working with an estate planning professional early on, he could have minimized family stress and prevented legal complications.

The Outcome: Because Mark never formalized his estate plan, his assets went through a lengthy and costly probate process. His children were forced to make decisions without knowing his exact wishes, leading to family disagreements. Meanwhile, financial accounts were frozen, and critical healthcare choices had to be made without his input.

The Lesson: Estate planning is about distributing wealth and protecting your loved ones from unnecessary stress and uncertainty. Life is unpredictable, and waiting too long can leave your family in a difficult position. Taking action now ensures that your wishes are honoured, your assets are protected, and your family is spared from legal and emotional burdens.

How to Approach the Conversation (for Parents and Adult Children)

Parent Starting the Conversation

Starting a conversation about estate planning can be delicate, but approaching it thoughtfully can help avoid misunderstandings and foster an open dialogue. Begin by choosing an appropriate time and setting—one that is calm, neutral, and free from distractions. Avoid bringing up the topic during emotionally charged moments, such as holidays or family gatherings, where stress levels may already be high. Instead, schedule a dedicated time to discuss your plans in a way that encourages open and honest dialogue.

A helpful approach is to express your reasons for having the conversation early on. You might say something like, "I want to make sure everything is clear and planned so that there's no confusion or stress later on. My goal is to ensure that our family's future is secure and that my wishes are known." This reassures your children that the discussion is about preparation, not control or favouritism.

Encourage questions and be open to feedback. Your children may have concerns about how certain assets are being distributed or how responsibilities are being assigned. Giving them a space to express their thoughts can help them feel heard and included, making them more likely to respect and support your decisions.

If the conversation becomes difficult or emotions run high, consider using a neutral third party, such as a financial advisor, estate planner, or mediator, to help guide the discussion. This can be particularly useful when there are complex financial assets, family businesses, or differing opinions among siblings.

Adult Children Starting the Conversation

Bringing up the topic of estate and real estate planning with parents can feel uncomfortable, but it's an important conversation to have before major decisions need to be made. Many adult children hesitate to ask about their parents' plans out of fear of seeming greedy or intrusive. However, approaching the discussion with genuine care and concern instead of focusing on financial details can help set the right tone. Framing the conversation around ensuring their wishes are honoured and avoiding potential stress or conflict among family members can make it easier for parents to open up.

Starting a conversation about estate planning as an adult child can feel awkward, especially if it hasn't been discussed before. Many adult children may be unsure of how to approach their parents about this sensitive subject. Directly asking about inheritance or what parents intend to do with their property can feel uncomfortable and put undue pressure on the parents. It's crucial to frame the conversation in a way that feels natural and opens the door for a discussion without creating feelings of discomfort.

Instead of jumping straight into asking about inheritance, an adult child can approach the conversation in a broader, more thoughtful way. A gentle opening might be: "Mom and Dad, I was reading about estate planning, and it made me realize we've never really talked about what you'd like to happen with your home in the future. Have you thought about it?"

This makes it about planning for the future and not about personal expectations. Sharing real-life examples can also help ease into the conversation: "A friend's family had a tough time deciding what to do with their parents' cottage because no one had talked about it ahead of time. I'd love to avoid that kind of situation for our family."

It's important to express concern rather than expectation: "I don't need to know details, but I just want to make sure we're prepared if something happens down the road."

By approaching the topic this way, the adult child can facilitate a conversation that feels less like an interrogation and more like a responsible discussion about future planning. The parents are less likely to feel pressured and more likely to engage openly about their wishes and thoughts. Showing concern for preparedness and using real-life examples makes it easier for parents to open up about their plans, ensuring a smoother and more constructive discussion.

Key Questions to Cover in The Family Meeting

When discussing estate planning, families should address several key topics to ensure clarity and prevent misunderstandings. First, it's important to decide what will happen to the family home.

- Will it be kept in the family, or is selling it a better option?

- If the property is kept, how will maintenance costs be shared among heirs?

Another important consideration is the potential tax implications.

- Who will be responsible for covering capital gains tax or property transfer taxes, and are there other taxes that may affect the estate or property?

Next, families should discuss how to handle situations where one child wants to keep the property.

- If one child wants to keep the property, how will the other heirs be compensated?

- Can siblings buy out the heir who wants to retain the property, or will other assets be distributed in a way that balances the decision?

If multiple heirs will co-own the property, it's wise to determine whether a trust or co-ownership agreement will be set up. If so, a formal agreement should be established to clearly outline responsibilities and usage rights.

Philanthropic or charitable bequests should also be addressed. If you wish to leave a portion of your estate to charity or a specific cause, discuss which organizations or charities will receive a donation, how much they will receive, and whether any particular conditions should be met. This ensures that your charitable intentions are clear and properly executed after your passing.

When discussing estate planning with family, go beyond the financial and logistical details, and acknowledge the emotional aspects involved. Real estate, inheritance, and charitable giving often carry deep personal meaning. A family home may hold decades of memories, and decisions about its future can bring up feelings of attachment, fairness, or even resentment. Taking the time to discuss the "why" behind your decisions—whether it's wanting to keep a property in the family, ensuring fairness among siblings, or supporting a cause that reflects your values—can help bring understanding and reduce potential conflicts. Encouraging family members to express their thoughts and emotions can foster a sense of transparency and trust, making the process smoother for everyone involved.

Lastly, you need to address estate tax planning. If the property is valuable, will life insurance or other assets be used to cover estate taxes, preventing the need to sell the home? Is there a plan in place to fund estate taxes without liquidating the family home? By covering these topics, families can ensure everyone is on the same page, avoid confusion, and minimize potential conflicts in the future.

Your Assets, Your Choice:
Avoid Outside Pressures

At the end of the day, your assets are your choice, and they represent a lifetime of hard work, values, and the future you envision for yourself and your family. The most important factor in any financial decision is ensuring that it aligns with **what truly matters to you.**

Anecdotally, I can tell you it makes very little tangible difference to your heirs whether they inherit $800,000 versus $700,000, $1.4 million versus $1.2 million, or even $7 million versus $6 million.

I see it time and time again—people spend years obsessing over their portfolios, optimizing every detail, only for everything to be sold to cash and divvied out after their passing. Their darling stocks, favourite rental property and prized collection of antique soda bottles all sold and spent on something else. The beneficiaries who had no connection to the process see it as just money, without any understanding of the time, effort, and purpose behind it.

That's why you should step back from the numbers and ask yourself: **What's important about money to me?** If you don't make those decisions intentionally, someone else will. A well-structured financial plan has empirical efficiency and ensures your wealth serves the right purpose, both now and for generations to come.

Key Takeaways

It's important to begin the conversation early before emotions run high or decisions are forced by health issues. The discussion should be approached with sensitivity. Parents should frame it as responsible planning, while children should avoid coming across as entitled and insensitive. Have a structured, open dialogue, rather than making assumptions or keeping matters secret. Consider bringing in outside advisors to help keep the conversation productive and objective. Finally, all decisions should be documented in writing to avoid legal disputes in the future.

"It is difficult to get a man to understand something when his salary depends on his not understanding it."
- Upton Sinclair.

Chapter 13:

Finding the Right Advisor for Your Wealth and Real Estate

Asset Management vs Wealth Management

It's important to understand a general distinction between asset management and wealth management. Most Canadians working with banks or financial advisors receive the service of asset management, focused on advice for investing liquid assets in isolation.

In contrast, wealth management takes a more comprehensive, team-based approach, endeavouring to offer advice across many aspects of your financial situation. All while partnering with your lawyers, accountants, and insurance specialists to include illiquid assets, tax strategies, and risk management relative to your values.

Why You Need a "Family CFO"

Over the years, I've built a trusted network of professionals across a wide range of industries including accountants, realtors, lawyers, tradespeople, financial specialists, and business advisors. Whether clients need a mortgage broker, estate planner, contractor, or even a personal trainer, I can connect them with reliable experts who align with their goals.

By fostering these relationships, I help clients navigate not just their financial future but the many transitions that come with family, real estate, retirement, and major life changes. Working alongside their existing financial professionals, we take a proactive approach to simplify complex decisions and make the process as seamless as possible.

How To Choose a Competent Financial Advisor

Going from real estate to retirement is a journey that requires careful planning and informed decision-making. One of the most critical steps in this journey is selecting a competent advisor who can guide you through the changing life stages.

A competent financial advisor can be instrumental in helping you achieve your financial goals. They can assist you in developing a personalized financial plan that is tailored to your unique values, risk tolerance, and time horizon. They can guide you through complex financial products, providing clarity on various investment options and their suitability for your specific goals. A financial advisor also helps you stay disciplined, maintaining focus on your long-term objectives, especially during periods of market volatility. Furthermore, they can steer you clear of common pitfalls, preventing impulsive decisions that could jeopardize your financial well-being.

Key Questions to Ask Before Working With Any Professional

When selecting an advisor in Canada, consider the following:

Registration and Regulation: Ensure the advisor is registered with the appropriate regulatory bodies in your province or territory. Registration confirms they meet specific professional standards and are authorized to offer financial advice.

Qualifications and Designations: Look for advisors with recognized credentials, such as:

- Certified Financial Planner (CFP): Indicates comprehensive financial planning expertise.

- Chartered Financial Analyst (CFA): Denotes a strong foundation in investment management.

- Personal Financial Planner (PFP): Signifies proficiency in personal financial planning.

These designations reflect a commitment to ongoing education and adherence to ethical standards.

Experience and Track Record: Inquire about the advisor's experience, areas of specialization, and typical clientele. Request references to assess their performance and client satisfaction.

Compensation Structure: Understand how the advisor is compensated: fee-only, commission-based, or a combination. Transparency in fees ensures alignment with your interests and helps prevent potential conflicts of interest.

Fiduciary Duty: Determine whether the advisor has a fiduciary obligation to act in your best interest. Advisors with a fiduciary duty are legally required to prioritize your needs above their own.

Services Offered: Clarify the scope of services provided, such as retirement planning, tax strategies, estate planning, or investment management, to ensure they align with your financial goals.

The author does not endorse or promote any specific financial advisor or firm. Readers are encouraged to conduct their own due diligence when selecting professionals.

"A ship is safest in the harbour,
but what is it made for?"
- John A. Shedd.

Conclusion:

Retire & Thrive on Your Terms

I didn't grow up thinking about retirement planning, tax strategies, or how to structure real estate as part of a long-term financial plan. I think like most people. These topics can seem overwhelming, complicated, or like something you'll deal with "someday." But over the years—both personally and professionally—I've seen firsthand how much is lost when we avoid these decisions and how much can be gained by facing them head-on with clarity and intention.

I've seen many wealthy people like Jake Miller, from the beginning of this book, feel anxious because they didn't understand how to turn what they had into reliable income. I've seen missed opportunities—avoidable tax bills, delayed decisions, family conflict—all because the pieces weren't being looked at together. And I've seen the relief and confidence that comes when everything finally clicks, which allows my clients to thrive when they realize they're in control of their plan, not the other way around.

That's what motivated me to write this book. Not just to share strategies but to help bridge that gap between complexity and clarity. Especially when it comes to real estate, which so often gets treated as an afterthought when, in reality, it's one of the most powerful financial tools many Canadians own.

As you reflect on the three stages of your real estate and retirement journey, consider this: Does your current advisor talk to you about more than just investments? Are they taking the time to discuss one of your largest assets—real estate—and offering guidance on how it fits into your family's hopes and dreams? Real estate is a powerful tool for wealth accumulation, but it needs to be treated with the same care and consideration as any other part of your investment portfolio. If your advisor isn't helping you navigate real estate as part of your broader financial picture, now might be the right time to seek the guidance you need.

Stage One: Pre-Retirement— Unlocking Your Wealth

During the pre-retirement phase, the goal is to optimize wealth creation. This is the stage where the value of real estate can help propel you toward your retirement goals. By using your property effectively, whether through appreciating asset value or rental income, you can enhance your overall portfolio, creating a more secure foundation for your retirement.

Stage Two: During Retirement—Simplify, Optimize and Create Cash Flow

In retirement, simplifying and ensuring steady cash flow becomes the focus. Real estate, particularly your primary residence and any rental properties, plays a key role in creating a consistent income stream. Whether you choose to downsize, rent out a portion of your home, or access home equity, these real estate decisions must align with your goal of enjoying a stable, predictable cash flow during retirement.

Stage Three: Estate Planning
—Keeping Real Estate in the Family (The Right Way)

Estate planning is the stage where a proactive approach to real estate is essential. By planning in advance, you can avoid unnecessary tax burdens, probate complications, and potential family conflicts. Whether through a trust, joint ownership, or a clearly structured will, ensuring that your real estate is passed down according to your wishes is key to preserving wealth for the next generation.

Never forget

While this book is designed to get you to rethink your real estate and financial planning, remember to start planning by understanding your value ladder first. Your values are the foundation upon which all your decisions should be built. Only by aligning your financial choices with what matters most to you can you make the best decisions for yourself, using the facts as they are. Ultimately, when your values are clear, the decision is easy.

Thank you so much for taking the time to read this book. Your support means more than words can express, and I am deeply grateful for your interest in the topics covered within these pages. I would also like to extend my heartfelt appreciation for the role you're playing in supporting an incredibly important cause. All profits from this book's sales are donated to the Victoria Women's Transition House, an organization dedicated to helping women and children escape and recover from domestic violence. By reading this book, you've contributed to their important work, and together, we're making a meaningful difference.

I also want to take a moment to express my thanks to all those who helped to review this book and provide me with valuable insights and feedback to make it more relatable and impactful and finally to give thanks and express gratitude to my wife, who has always been my number one supporter and pushes me to always become more. Without her inspiration, love, and belief in me, this book would not have been possible. Thank you to her, and all of you, for helping bring this vision to life and making a lasting impact in the world.